ALSO BY DANIEL HUDON

The Bluffer's Guide to the Cosmos

Evidence for Rainfall

The Hole in the Kitchen Floor

BRIEF EULOGIES for LOST ANIMALS

An Extinction Reader

by DANIEL HUDON

Lynn,
Hope you enjoy these sad
stories. It's great to
know you!
All the best,
Daniel Hudon

Pen & Anvil

ACKNOWLEDGEMENTS. Excerpts from this collection have appeared in the journals *Canary*, *Chattahoochee Review*, *Clarion*, *Entropy Magazine*, *Flyway*, *The Goose*, *Paragraphiti*, *Riprap*, *Toad*, and *Zoomorphic*, and in the volume *{Ex}tinguished and {Ex}tinct: An Anthology of Things That No Longer {Ex}ist* (Twelve Winters Press).

ISBN: 978-0991622283
Printed in the United States of America.

Published in 2017 by the Pen & Anvil Press, an imprint of the Boston Poetry Union. Permissions inquiries may be sent by post to PO Box 15274, Boston, Massachusetts 02215, or by email via *www.penandanvil.com*.

Project editor, Zachary Bos, with the editorial assistance of Natalie Janes. The text in this collection is set in the Minion typeface, with headings in Egyptian and Monoline Script. Cover design and interior layout by Darby Thompson.

FOREWORD

There is a strange contradiction in that humankind, whose art and ritual and song celebrates nature with such emotion, has been the major cause for the massive loss of species in the modern era. We love and destroy the creatures that share the planet with us.

Daniel Hudon's eulogies may, in their first lines, strike the reader like a poetic celebration of the diversity of the zoological world. Life's imagination seems semi-magical and infinite in its inventiveness as we encounter delightful animals with fairy-tale names: the Pig-footed Bandicoot, the Dodo, the Gastric-brooding frog, the Turquoise-throated Puffleg.

For a moment these enchanted names transport into a dreamy world of vast natural diversity. But we are, in fact, poised unknowingly on a cusp between delight and doom. That is the subtle trick of this book. Having been lulled by the author's careful, loving descriptions, in which animals appear still to live on their own terms, we are, at the turn of a sentence, confronted with their vanishing.

Size of animal and geographical situation will determine that an insect here, a mouse there, disappears in a tiny, solitary last breath, imperceptible to us in the long chronology of the world, only to be later found out accidentally. By contrast, the obliteration of other species occurs in full observance, convoyed by the sullen pomp of an exhaustive list of factors and their interwoven, apparently inevitable and fatal process. In this case, the tone is sometimes terse and thereby brutal. For, directly or indirectly, the causes of extinction originate in mankind.

This book breeds nostalgia and seems, tacitly, to acknowledge it as one of the prime failures of the human psyche to value what is rare or no longer there. The close relationship of inspiration between art, poetry and those animals that once were, no longer exists. The dwindling number of actors and of natural abundance on earth seems to foretell a stage of life, or non-life, as empty as in the Samuel Beckett's *Waiting for Godot*—a depiction of the acting-out of existence reduced to melancholic dialogue.

But through these eulogies the book also, in a way, brings the species back to life, reasserts their kinship with our world and with us, having once been contemporaries of ours. By at first presenting them in their native and undisturbed environment, the author sets them on an equal footing with our own species, implies that, like us, they have personalities and individual destinies, as so convincingly promulgated by Konrad Lorenz in his book *King Solomon's Ring*.

Species extinction through our doings acquires, consequently, something of the quality of murder.

The principal underlying message is that by saving other species than our own, and allowing them to live as they are entitled to on this planet, we save ourselves from the terrible solitude of our intellect and preserve and enrich our scientific and artistic potential.

As suggested by Rupert Sheldrake in *The Rebirth of Nature*, the greater the variety of species on earth, the greater our enchantment in the world. The way to it is to re-instill sacredness in all forms of life, as once was the case, thereby restraining that peculiar human paradox which is to lead a species to extinction for the very reason that we admire it or find it useful to us. Our happiness and, ultimately, our own survival depends on theirs.

What Daniel Hudon so cogently reminds us with this gathering of brief elegies, eulogies, is that the loss of each species is accompanied by the loss of another portion of our humanity.

STEPHANIE V. SEARS
Marblehead, Mass.

INTRODUCTION

"Forgetting is another kind of extinction," artist Todd McGrain said to me when I interviewed him in 2012.* For more than a decade he has been creating larger-than-life sculptures of birds formerly common in North America, such as the passenger pigeon, to memorialize them. "These birds are not commonly known," he has written elsewhere, "and they ought to be… It's such a thorough erasing."

Since the year 1500, no fewer than nine hundred species have become extinct. Are their stories being told? This loss is a crisis in human values, as our relatives on the tree of life are disappearing under our watch and because of our actions. Aside from a few high profile extinctions, like the passenger pigeon and the dodo, most lost species are unknown to the general public, and the danger of forgetting part of our biological heritage is great. There are no historical parallels here. Aldo Leopold said, "For one species to mourn another is a new thing under the sun."

The recent animal extinctions include twenty-eight reptiles, thirty-four amphibians, sixty-three fish, sixty-three insects, ninety-two mammals, one hundred and sixty-six birds and more than three hundred mollusks. Who are these animals? Where did they live? What do we know of their biology and natural history? Each animal had its own evolutionary history, ecological niche and characteristics that made it a unique form of life. But they have disappeared from the Earth due to our actions and without proper recognizance. The beginning of wisdom, the Chinese say, is to call things by their rightful names. In many cases, the names are known by scientists and what little is known of the animal's habits is hidden away in scientific papers. These details need to be brought to light to make the species come alive, at least in our imagination, to help bring the enormity of what has and is happening within our grasp.

Evidence abounds that the present species extinction rate is more than one thousand times the historical rate measured in the fossil record—an indication that we are in a mass extinction. Life on Earth has seen five mass extinctions, the most recent being sixty-five million years ago when the dinosaurs were wiped out. This sixth extinction is human-caused with habitat alteration, over-exploitation, introduction of invasive species and pollution the major factors.

Naturalist William Beebe wrote in 1906 that "when the last individual of a race of living beings breathes no more, another heaven and another earth must pass before such a one can be again." Our heaven exists now and by memorializing and celebrating what is now gone, we can perhaps keep what we still have.

I'd like to thank the many scientists and experts who answered questions and sent files or research papers over the several years I've spent working on this book, including Paul Brock (National History Museum, London), Sheila Conant (University of Hawaii at Manoa), Exequiel Ezcurra (University of California, Riverside), Garth Foster (Balfour-Browne Club and the Aquatic Coleoptera Conservation Trust, Ayr, Scotland), Frank Howarth (Bishop Museum, Hawaii), Les Kaufman (Boston University), Roger Lederer (California State University, Chico), lepidopterist Liam O'Brien (San Francisco), Claire Regnier (Muséum National d'Histoire Naturelle, Paris), Ignacio Ribera (Institut de Biologia Evolutiva, Barcelona), and Chris Schneider (Boston University).

DANIEL HUDON
Boston, Mass.

* This interview can be found online at at *www.penandanvil.com/brief-eulogies.*

Contents

I. LOST ANIMALS OF NORTH AMERICA

II. LOST ANIMALS OF HAWAII AND THE PACIFIC ISLANDS

III. LOST ANIMALS OF CENTRAL AND SOUTH AMERICA

IV. LOST ANIMALS OF EUROPE

V. LOST ANIMALS OF AUSTRALIA AND NEW ZEALAND

VI. LOST ANIMALS OF ASIA

VII. LOST ANIMALS OF AFRICA

VIII. LOST ANIMALS OF THE INDIAN OCEAN

BRIEF EULOGIES for LOST ANIMALS

Not long ago, within the last two centuries, few people imagined a species could become extinct. Now few can imagine there can be so many that have vanished.

* * *

"Extinction," from the Latin *stinguere,* "to quench," as a flame. Diane Ackerman writes in *The Rarest of the Rare*: "we have long been obsessed with the notion of fires within our own bodies… When we say something is extinct, we mean literally that the flame in each and every cell has been doused."

The *Oxford English Dictionary* quotes several past uses of the word. From Prescott's *History of the Reign of Ferdinand and Isabella,* 1838:

> The sudden extinction of those hopes which she had so long cherished.

From Thomas Carlyle's *Reminiscences,* 1871:

> A bright lamp flickering out into extinction.

And from Alfred Russell Wallace's *Island Life,* 1880:

> The most effective agent in the extinction of species is the pressure of other species.

Though Wallace, Darwin's contemporary and the co-originator of the theory of evolution, meant other *animal* species, today the greatest extinction agent is pressure from humans.

* * *

No continent has undergone such a massive population change and landscape alteration in such a short time as North America. The effect on the resident species has been disastrous.

According to the International Union for the Conservation of Nature (IUCN), the continental United States has the most extinct species, at one hundred and fifty-five.

I.
Lost Animals of
North America

"We ourselves are the subject of a breathtaking new chapter in the cosmic biography: the emergence of a life form—*Homo sapiens*—able to reflect with insight and wonder upon life itself in all its infinite dimensions. A bat will never know the astonishing thing that it is. Nor will a crow or an ant or a sloth. Humans stand alone among all living things on Earth—and perhaps in the universe—in this gift of being able to appreciate every species for its uniqueness."

– Edward McCord, "The Value of Species,"
National Parks Magazine, 2013

Ainsworth's Salamander
Plethodon ainsworthi

After the Atlantic Ocean first began to grow, long before *Tyrannosaurus rex* came and went, before flowers ever began to bloom, the ancestor of Ainsworth's salamander lost its lungs and began to breathe through its skin. This happened over many generations for reasons that are still being debated by biologists. Eventually, as the Appalachians rose, fell, and rose again, lungless salamanders diversified into more than four hundred species, each finding damp, humid areas to keep their skin moist, often hiding under rocks or in crevices and only coming out at night.

In 1964, Harold Ainsworth collected two salamanders two miles south of Bay Springs, Mississippi, in "springhead litter" on the forest floor. He initially labeled them *Plethodon glutinosus*, the northern slimy salamander, and they wound up in a drawer in the Mississippi Museum of Natural Science. Twenty-seven years later, in 1991, James Lazell found them, recognized their slender bodies as being peculiarly long, and described them as a new species, *Plethodon ainsworthi*. Lazell went back to the same place year after year to collect more, and though he found other salamanders, he never again found any *P. ainsworthi* individuals. In his 1998 paper, in which he first described the species, he remarked on the clear-cutting and destruction of trees in the area for wood-chipping: "It is impossible to guess how many small, cryptic species may have been lost already and difficult to believe we can move quickly enough even to save this one, now that it is known." The impressive evolutionary lineage of *P. ainsworthi* appears to have been terminated.

Under the Conservation Actions heading on the IUCN Redlist's entry for *P. ainsworthi*, the text reads, with scientific finality: "There are no conservation measures needed; this species is extinct."

The Amistad Gambusia
Gambusia amistadensis

Named for the Cuban term *gambusino*, which means to be so small as to signify nothing. If you are fishing for gambusinos—minnows little more than an inch long—the joke goes, you are catching nothing.

Amistad gambusias were mosquitofish that lived only in Good-enough Spring, part of the Rio Grande drainage in Texas. When the spring was inundated with silt-laden water after the creation of the Amistad Reservoir in 1968, the Amistad gambusia disappeared.

Now, truly, if you are fishing for gambusinos, you are catching nothing.

Bachman's Warbler
Vermivora bachmanii

At times the insect-like song of the elusive songbird seemed to emanate from all round, as if the trees themselves were singing, but investigation invariably showed the bird sitting motionless upon the same limb. Often it was heard from the tip of a sweet gum or cypress in the pale and gloomy woods and bottomland swamps of the southeastern states, and after leaving a tree it would fly a great distance before alighting again. Impossible to follow through the dark forest, it could only be detected by its song. Males were mostly yellow, with olive green on the upper parts, females were olive above and yellowish below, and both had black eyes and dark bills. Females could rarely be disturbed while incubating the eggs, and both took part in feeding the young. Only the male sang; the female had no song.

The Banff Longnose Dace
Rhinichthys cataractae smithi

Suspended among rocks and reeds; hiding, darting about to avoid being eaten; foraging at night. It isn't easy being a minnow, especially when your universe is a single marsh fed by a pair of hot springs in Banff National Park. Between the chlorine leaching in from the pools and the introduction into your warm waters of tropical fish—to eat mosquito larvae or just to look at from the boardwalk—who compete for food with you and eat your annually spawned eggs, you know your days are numbered.

The Birds of Guadalupe

Off the coast of Baja California, in the deep clear waters that surround Guadalupe Island, great white sharks hunt for prey. On the island's rocky shores, elephant and fur seals flop and rest. On the denuded flanks of the dormant volcanoes small groves of cypress and palm trees stand against the incessant winds.

The invasion of the goats is over. Brought by whalers and sealers for food on their return journeys the last goats were removed a few years ago, but not before exacting supreme damage. In grazing the island down to stone, they destroyed the habitat of the ground-nesting birds, who were then preyed upon by feral cats.

* * *

The Guadalupe storm petrel (*Oceanodrama macrodactyla*), a black seabird with webbed feet who roamed freely over the oceans and only sought the island to breed, is gone.

The Guadalupe Bewick's wren (*Thryomanus bewickii brevicauda*), a small brown bird with a long tail and a loud elaborate song, is gone.

The Guadalupe spotted towhee (*Pipilo maculates consobrinus*), a large sparrow with a black head, white spots on its black wings and a dark, rusty-colored body—and who did a comical "bunny hop" as it foraged among the leaf litter for food—is gone.

The Guadalupe caracara (*Caracara lutosus*), a tropical falcon that looked and behaved like a vulture, lived peacefully on the island until the goatherds, who managed some 50,000 goats, decided it was a threat to the kids and hunted them to the brink of extinction. Museum collectors, interested in this now rare bird, finished them off. Among the few detailed descriptions of the living quelilis, as they were called, in 1875 one ornithologist noted, "When surprised or wounded, they utter a loud, harsh scream something like a bald eagle." This is a sound that has not been heard on Guadalupe for more than a century.

* * *

Something of the character of the quelili is revealed in this anecdote of W.E. Bryant, a museum collector, who visited the island in 1887. Bryant shot a male and noted that the badly wounded bird was determined to exit with dignity. At first, the quelili

> attempted to escape by running, with the assistance of his wings. Being over-taken and brought to bay, instead of throwing himself on his back in an attitude of defense, or uttering a cry for quarter, he raised his crest and with an air of defiance, calmly awaited death.

Notes on the Guadalupe Storm Petrel

FIVE PHOTOS: lateral view (left), lateral view (right), ventral view (two positions), dorsal view. Wings straight down at its sides, as if plummeting into oblivion, inch-long beak hooked slightly downwards, a glass bead for an eye, black feathers except for a few white ones on its rump. (Forked tail not visible.) Altogether no bigger than a robin.

A TAG TIED TO ITS FOOT: catalogue #6885. *Oceanodroma macrodactyla.* Collected by Beck/Anthony 3-24-1897.

OCEANODROMA: 'runner on the ocean'.

MACRODACTYLA: 'large fingers', referring to its webbed feet.

PETREL: diminutive of Peter, the saint who walked on water. The bird's ability to hover over water, sometimes letting its legs dangle in, gave the appearance of walking.

STORM-PETREL: lives at sea, beyond the horizon. Approaches land when storms threaten, often sheltering in the lee of ships, hence known as harbingers of doom.

GUADALUPE STORM-PETREL: inhabited the Pacific winds off Baja. Only sought the island of Guadalupe for nesting

HABITS: avoided avian predators by landing at night, its black feathers invisible in the dark. Known to nest in burrows, otherwise behaviors unknown.

CALLS: recent reports of calling at night raise hope it survives, but no other evidence exists.

THREATS: degradation of habitat on Guadalupe by introduced goats (numbering up to one hundred thousand), now removed, and predation by feral cats, also removed.

CLASSIFICATION: critically endangered, possibly extinct. Not seen since 1912.

FROM "SONG OF THE STORM-PETREL" BY MAXIM GORKY:

> Above the gray plain of the sea, the wind gathers storm-clouds.
> Between the clouds and the sea soars the storm-petrel, like a streak
> of black lightning.

The Caribbean Monk Seal
Neomonachus tropicalis

Like a sort of mermaid, they hauled themselves up onto empty beaches to bask in the sun and rest. They did this on isolated atolls and islands. Sometimes they did it in groups of twenty or forty and would lie about like old men, feeling the warm breeze on their whiskers. They made seclusion their paradise, molted here and birthed here. It was a paradise devoid of sugarcane machinery or fisherman's lamps. Playful, curious and unafraid of humans, they were easily slaughtered.

The waves of the sea came and went and the conch shells cast upon the shore recorded their sighs.

The Carolina Parakeet
Conuropsis carolinensis

On cold winter days when snow buried the land, a streak of green would alight from the sky and descend upon the barren branches of a large sycamore tree. When the sun shone brightly upon the inhabited tree top, the many yellow heads looked like so many candles, like a kind of Christmas tree.

*   *   *

One of the tragic habits of the Carolina parakeet was for the flock to sweep repeatedly around a wounded or dead companion, squawking and screeching until they too fell to the hunter.

*   *   *

In midsummer, with the tree fully leafed out, flying with such a boisterous din, the birds would all pitch into the tree and become silent. So great had been the din just a second before; and now, green within green, they disappeared into the tree, leaving a bewildering stillness.

The Coquis of Puerto Rico
Eleutherodactylus spp.

At night, the male coqui sings for his mate. He sings from the trees, from mountain streams and waterfalls, from lowland mud-banks and from inside bromeliads. Sometimes, in his singing, he duels another male in a territorial sing-off. All over Puerto Rico, from dusk till dawn, you can hear the two-note song of this tiny tree frog. It is a lullaby for the locals, who fall asleep to the chorus, the subject of songs and poems, paintings and petroglyphs, a symbol for the island and a badge of honor: *I'm as Puerto Rican as a coqui*, they say. The quickest way to make a Puerto Rican homesick is to imitate the high-pitched call: *ko-kee, ko-kee.*

But the choir is losing some of its voices. The web-footed coqui, *E. karlschmidti*, one of the largest species on the island, hasn't been heard since 1974. The golden coqui, *E. jasperi*, no bigger than a dime, lived hidden in the base of bromeliads; it hasn't been heard since 1981. The little-known mottled coqui, *E. eneida*, hasn't been heard since 1990.

The Last Dusky Seaside Sparrow
Ammodramus maritimus nigrescens

In the jar, all is quiet. It can't hear anything. No traffic, no mosquitoes, no rockets blasting off to the moon. The air is pure though sadly, the wind never blows. The marsh is long gone.

Its blind eye lies open, unseeing in its green glossiness. Its head is pressed against the bottom of the jar, yellow beak closed, mottled feathers tussled. Just an ounce of bird, the few notes of its song unsung. A tag on its claw reads:

Dusky "Orange"
Last one
Died 18 Jun 87

The Flight of the Eskimo Curlews
Numenius borealis

Once the curlews flew across North America in vast flocks a mile long and a hundred yards wide. From far off the calls of a distant flock were said to sound like the jingling of countless sleigh bells. They flew in a wedge shape, the sides of which constantly swayed back and forth like a cloud of smoke wafted by the lightest wind. At times, the leader would plunge downwards successively, followed by the rest in a graceful undulation, clumping for a moment into a dense mass and splaying into a thin sheet spread wide, forming and reforming like a great shifting cloud.

Strong fliers, theirs was among the greatest migrations of any living creature, wrapping the Americas in a giant elliptical ribbon, from their breeding grounds high in the Canadian Arctic to their wintering spot in the Argentinean pampas and back. Southbound, they stopped in Labrador where the Cree named them *weekemenesew*, meaning "likes eating berries." On a visit there in 1833, John James Audubon observed them arriving, "flock after flock... in search of the feeding grounds, [flying] in close masses, sometimes high, at other times low, but always with remarkable speed, and performing beautiful evolutions in the air."

After alighting they all ran the same direction, probing the low bushes with their four-inch bills and picking up the berries in their way. They plumped up so much that by the time they flew down the East Coast, hunters named them "dough birds."

In one of Audubon's illustration for his landmark tome The Birds of America, a male curlew laments his fallen mate. Such a scene was common, whether the birds were flying south or north. In The Last of the Curlews, Fred Bodsworth quotes a 19th century bulletin: "They were so confiding, so full of sympathy for their fallen companions that in closely packed ranks they fell, easy victims of the carnage." In Bodsworth's tale, a male curlew's solo flight is interrupted when he finally finds a mate. After a brief, exhilarating courtship, she succumbs to a hunter's shot and the male flies on alone.

No Eskimo curlews have been seen since the mid-1980s.

The Great Auk
Pinguinis impennis

Among the islands and skerries of the North Atlantic Ocean once thrived the great auk, a seabird the size of a large goose. Known as *isarokitsoq* ("stump-winged") by the Greenlandic Inuit and *geirfugl* ("spearbird," referring to its large bill) by the Norse, the great auk was unable to fly and awkward on land, but a strong swimmer that "easily left a six-oared boat far behind." It was capable of accelerating under water then shooting itself above the ocean's surface onto an island ledge. Otherwise, it would swim up to rocky outcroppings and hop ashore to find a mate and breed.

Some of the larger colonies probably numbered tens of thousands of birds. Males and females were thought to mate for life. When she was ready, the female laid a single pear-shaped egg directly onto the rocks. Eggs had unique markings as if brown ink had been drizzled over them, perhaps so their parents could recognize them in the crowded colonies.

A companion of humans for millennia, the great auk was hunted by Neanderthals one hundred thousand years ago and painted onto caves in Spain thirty-five thousand years ago. In the early 1500s, Jacques Cartier was astounded by the colony on Funk Island, off Newfoundland:

> numbers are so great as to be incredible, unless one has seen them;
> for although the island is about a league in circumference, it is
> so exceedingly full of birds that one would think they had been
> stowed there.

Sighted far beyond these rocky outposts, great auks provided a valuable navigation aid for fishing ships that land was near. Initially, they were hunted for fresh meat, oil and eggs, as, Cartier adds, "these birds are so fat it is marvelous," but when auks replaced eider as the down of choice, their fate was sealed. With their numbers plummeting in the 1700s from overhunting, the extinction warnings went unheeded and scientists and museum collectors scrambled to get one before it was too late. The last pair of great auks were strangled off Iceland in 1844 while incubating an egg.

A Vole-shaped Hole on Gull Island
Microtus nesophilus

> Where has he gone, my meadow mouse,
> My thumb of a child that nuzzled in my palm?
> – Theodore Roethke, "The Meadow Mouse"

On Great Gull Island, a 17-acre glacial moraine off the eastern point of Long Island, once lived the Gull Island vole, who had a brown coat and a dusky underbelly washed with cinnamon. Named *nesophilus*, or "island-lover," this meadow mouse ran rampant on the island, preventing a lighthouse keeper from growing much in his garden.

After 1898, when the US government built Fort Michie on the island and covered much of it with cement, the Gull Island vole disappeared.

The Harelip Sucker
Moxostoma lacerum

The harelip sucker once lived in eight different eastern-central states, in pools of clear-water streams that ran over rocky or gravel bottoms. Named for its peculiar mouth and lips—it had a fixed upper lip and a lower lip split into two distinct lobes—the harelip sucker fed on snails, limpets, fingernail clams and crustaceans. It likely held shells in the front of its mouth and sucked out the insides.

In the 19th century, as the population in the United States grew, forests were cut and land was cleared for agriculture. Because of the increased silt load, streams that had been clear became cloudy and turbid. The silt smothered the mollusks and crustaceans that lived on the stream bottoms—the sucker's main food—and reduced its visibility to feed. The harelip sucker was last collected in 1893 and became the first fish to be declared extinct in North America.

The Heath Hen
Tympanuchus cupido cupido

A hollow hooting sound, like the subdued and distant echo of a tugboat tooting in the fog. A wailing of the wind spirit. A blowing in the neck of a bottle that carries further than a gunshot.

How else to describe the mating calls of the male heath hens when they gathered on the ancestral mating grounds each spring?

A vital, virile expression of the fecundity of old Mother Earth that could be heard a mile away. A booming.

Relatives of the prairie chicken, they were plump, short-tailed birds with vertical brown and white stripes and dangling neck feathers that could be raised into a v-shape when they were ready to show off. They puffed up the air sacs on their necks till they were as large as oranges, bowed their heads, raised their neck feathers like rabbit ears and charged one another in comical stutter steps, booming all the way.

As much a dance as a joust, the goal was to impress and intimidate, not to vanquish, so contact was rare. They veered off or jumped and spun half-circles in the air, challenging all creation, before landing and carrying on in the opposite direction. They paced about, as if summoning the courage to fight, and leapt over one another. Among the incessant booming, they cackled and laughed, the field becoming an absurd visual and oratory fiesta for the dawn hours, with a repeat at dusk.

Into the fray of strutting and bowing, some females went about their business, calm and unconcerned, pecking here and there for a grain of corn. Sometimes a male took a brief run towards a female, body inclined forward, tail feathers erect, circling this way and that, stamping, stamping, the field resonating with the drumming of feet.

The Ivory-billed Woodpecker
Campephilus principalis

"Nature's exclamation point, / the personification of pizzazz – / a full-throated yell of a bird." This was how Chris Cokinos described the ivory-billed, largest woodpecker in North America. Such was its size and majesty that sightings typically inspired exclamations of "Lord God!" and this became one of its nicknames, the Lord God Bird.

Black bodied with a white racing stripe that ran down its head and neck along its back, the ivory-billed had a gleaming yellow eye and was topped with a brilliant scarlet crest. Nearly two feet long from head to tail, it hopped up and down the sides of cypresses and hackeberries in search of a place to pound its three-inch-long bill into the bark for grubs of the long-horned beetle, its favorite food. Its call was tinny but extraordinarily loud, "like someone blowing into a megaphone with the mouthpiece of a clarinet, blasting out single notes that could be heard half a mile away."

You had to go scouting deep into the swamps and bottomlands that once spanned the deep South if you wanted to glimpse this famous recluse. How far did it roam for food? Did it have enemies? What were its courtship rituals? Did pairs mate for life? The high profile sightings couldn't answer these questions. It was only in the early part of the 20th century, with its numbers dwindling due to logging, that the State of Louisiana finally began to manage the last remaining habitat of the ivory-billed woodpecker. But the logging rights to the land were held by the Chicago Mill and Lumber Company, who refused to deal. "We are just money grubbers," admitted James F. Griswold, the chairman of the board for Chicago Mill. "We are not concerned, as are you folks, with ethical considerations." The land was logged in the 1940s, probably taking this charismatic woodpecker with it.

Today, the ivory-billed haunts birdwatchers, who from time to time report hearing the characteristic distant double knocks, and share grainy photos and stories of fleeting glimpses. Hope is high that "nature's exclamation" has not been muted, but evidence is slim.

The Labrador Duck
Camptorhynchus labradorius

Little is known of the Labrador duck. Its breeding and mating habits, migration routes, nesting and biology all went unstudied. Perhaps they nested on small, rocky islets off the coast of Labrador. Perhaps on islands in the Gulf of St. Lawrence. No one described the call of the bird.

It was known to taste poorly, with a strong flavor of shellfish. Its bill was colorful: orange with a blue-black tip. The males had a striking black body with black and white wings, a white neck and head topped by a black patch. The female was gray-brown, had white on her wings and a light line behind her eye.

Naturalists disagree on whether the bird was trusting or wary. They also disagree on whether the last one was shot in 1871, 1875 or 1878.

Lake Hadley Sticklebacks
Gasterosteus spp.

In biological circles, this pair of fish species were budding stars. Inhabiting tiny glacial lakes in the Gulf Islands of British Columbia, they were among Earth's youngest new species to evolve. They descended from the marine threespine stickleback (*G. aculeatus*), a minnow-like fish that swims into inland rivers and lakes to mate and reproduce.

When the ice sheets receded 13,000 years ago, sticklebacks ventured into new streams and, rather than returning to the sea, some young stayed along the bottoms of the lakes to complete their life cycles. There they remained when changing sea levels cut off the lakes.

When connection to the ocean was restored, a new wave of sticklebacks invaded, but enough time had passed that they didn't see the remnants of the first wave as potential mates any longer. The second-wave sticklebacks that stayed exploited the vacant, shallow water niche of the lakes. Still in the process of speciating, the two species don't even have unique names yet; they are simply referred to as '*Gasterosteus* spp.', and labeled according to their preferred water depth—the benthic species sticking to the bottom, and the limnetic species inhabiting the open shallows.

In the spring, male sticklebacks lose their camouflage colors and develop brilliant red neck spots and enticing blue eyes to attract mates. They scoop out small trench-like nests and when a female approaches, her abdomen swollen with eggs, the male darts about excitedly in a zig-zag pattern to impress her. If she responds, he shows her the opening to the nest, and she deposits her eggs that the male then protects.

But... the males were ill-equipped to protect the eggs at night. In the early 1990s, catfish were accidentally introduced to Lake Hadley. Being nocturnal bottom-feeders, they wiped out the next generation of sticklebacks. By 1995, one of evolution's greatest contemporary debuts was brought to a premature end.

The Little Swan Island Hutia
Geocapromys thoracatus

Through the cactus thickets and jagged fissures of the uplifted coraline limestone, the gray-brown hutia emerges, slow and guinea-pig-like, to forage on bark, leaves and small living things. Often it seeks the edge of the cliffs on this tiny rugged island to browse the profusion of wild vine. When it has time, it finds its mate. They wrestle playfully, sometimes aggressively, leaving fierce bite marks on each other's ears.

The hutia ruled its island unchallenged since the last ice age. A living specimen was once taken to be shown in audience before King Edward VII of England and before the king's dog. There it was remarked, with British understatement, the hutia "exhibited not the faintest signs of fear or suspicion in the presence of the dog or even of awe in the presence of His Majesty."

The Maryland Darter
Ethostoma sellare

Darters are bottom-dwelling fish, related to perch and walleye, that move quickly from beneath rocks, which is how they got their name. The Maryland darter liked to cluster in small groups in the part of Deer Creek where the water tumbles out of the hills onto the flatter coastal plain. It made its home in the last riffle before the flatlands.

Yellow-bodied with four distinguishing black saddle-bands, the Maryland darter fed on snails and insects. Though its mating habits were unknown, after the female spawned, males were known to guard the eggs. At the end of its life, the Maryland darter struggled against damming, increased sedimentation and urbanization. It has not been seen since the late 1980s.

The Freshwater Mussels of North America

Lolling about in the riffles and shallows of the Tennessee and Cumberland river systems were once so many mussels, their names evocative and flamboyant: sugarspoons and acornshells, winged spikes and narrow catspaws. The formerly free-flowing waters were filtered by angled riffleshells, forkshells, and leafshells, both Cumberland and plain, and in the gravels with rapid currents hid the yellow-blossoms, green-blossoms and tubercled-blossom pearly mussels.

Pollywogging in the Wabash tributaries would turn up abundant round combshells, Tennessee riffleshells and Sampson's naiads.

In the Apalachicola system, both the Chattahoochee and Flint Rivers that ran through the loblolly pine forests, you could find the lined pocketbook.

The hazel pigtoe reclined in the Mobile basin with the true pigtoe, while the Scioto pigtoe took to the Ohio and the Coosa elktoe to the Coosa.

The Carolina elktoe thrived in the Carolinas and the Ochlockonee arcmussel sought the shoals of the Ochlockonee River in Florida and Georgia.

The Tombigbee River has lost its eponymous moccasinshell, the Rio Grande its monkeyface and false spike. The empty valves of the stirrupshell were last collected in Alabama and Mississippi in 1989, their lustrous interiors still brilliant.

The Passenger Pigeon
Ectopistes migratorius

"For one species to mourn the death of another is a new thing under the sun," Aldo Leopold said in 1947 upon the dedication of a plaque to the passenger pigeon at Wisconsin's Wyalusing State Park, near the confluence of the Wisconsin and Mississippi Rivers. He once called the bird "a biological storm," and described trees that were "shaken by a living wind." According to Chief Pokagon of the Potawatomi tribe, the sound of the birds was "a mingling of sleigh bells, mixed with the rumbling of an approaching storm." John James Audubon estimated that a flock about one mile wide and one hundred eighty miles long took three hours to pass overhead and contained a billion members. He described another flock that took three days to pass.

Slightly larger than a mourning dove, with similar but more iridescent plumage, the passenger pigeon was the world's most abundant bird in the 19th century, but by the 1890s, a century of hunting had reduced the species to a few scattered individuals.

Remarking on the swiftness of the bird in flight, Audubon wrote, perhaps prophetically:

> When an individual is seen gliding through the woods and close to the observer, it passes like a thought, and on trying to see it again, the eye searches in vain; the bird is gone.

The Rocky Mountain Locust
Melanoplus spretus

For five days in 1875, the Rocky Mountain locust streamed overhead in a plague of biblical proportions—a swarm eighteen hundred miles long and at least one hundred and ten miles wide. The largest congregation of animal life ever recorded, this superorganism of 3.5 trillion insect bodies eclipsed the sun for days.

In *On the Banks of Plum Creek*, Laura Ingalls Wilder wrote:

> The cloud was hailing grasshoppers, the cloud was grasshoppers. Their bodies hid the sun and made darkness. Their thin, large wings gleamed and glittered. The rasping, whirring of their wings filled the whole air and they hit the ground and the house with the noise of a hailstorm.

The locusts ate everything from hanging laundry to wooden axe handles. They even chewed the wool right off the sheep. But twenty years later, they were all gone.

The Rocky Mountain locust is the only pest that has been driven to extinction, probably because of the cultivation of the soil of their breeding ground. It was an important food source for the Eskimo curlew, which eventually followed it into extinction.

The last locust was seen in 1902.

The Sea Mink
Neovison macrodon

According the Iroquois creation story, in the beginning, when the whole world was covered in water, the sea mink swam down to the bottom of the ocean to retrieve some soil. But the bottom of the ocean was so far away that the sea mink died in the attempt and floated up to the surface. When the other animals saw this, they noticed that he had some soil still clutched in its paws. This they spread on the back of a turtle, which was supporting the world, and it soon grew into the first island.

* * *

The sea mink spent most of its time in the water off the rocky coasts of New England and the Canadian Maritimes. Hunted for its pelt by Native Americans, the knockout blow was delivered when the sea mink was discovered by European fur traders. It was last seen in the 1880s, before it was properly studied or appreciated.

* * *

An account from Daniel Beard's *Fading Trails: The Story of Endangered American Wildlife* indicates how doggedly mink were pursued as the price paid for their skins rose:

> Some of these men went from island to island, hunting any small ledge where mink could live. They carried their dogs with them, and besides guns, shovels, pick axes and crow bars, took a good supply of pepper and brimstone. If they took refuge in holes or cracks of the ledges, they were usually dislodged by working with shovels and crow bars, and the dogs caught them when they came out. If they were in the crevices of the rocks where they could not be got at and their eyes could be seen to shine, they were shot and pulled out by means of an iron rod with a screw at the end. If they could not be seen, they were usually driven out by firing in charges of pepper. If this failed, then they were smoked with brimstone, in which case they either came out or were suffocated in their holes.

The Tecopa Pupfish
Cyprinodon nevadensis calidae

Beneath the Mojave Desert, magma churns. Through a fissure in the crust, the heat seethes up and stokes the Tecopa Hot Springs, remnants from the Pleistocene when the Mojave was full of lakes. As the lakes dried, some fish lingered, trapped in small pools and springs where water still seeped in from the ground. Only an inch long, the Tecopa pupfish evolved to thrive in the salty thermal springs, basking in water temperatures that hovered between 32 and 36 degrees Celsius.

In mating, male pupfish doggedly pursue females and snuggle up to them like puppies at play, giving the fish their name. In the Tecopa Hot Springs, this tiny fish lived undisturbed since the last great ice age. But when bathhouses were constructed, new channels into the pools increased their temperatures beyond what the fish could handle. Soon after, the Tecopa pupfish vanished.

The Tecopa pupfish was delisted from the Endangered Species Act in 1981, the first species to be removed from the list due to extinction.

Urania Sloanus at Sunrise

When the pear tree blossoms, one after another begins to appear just as the sun rises—*whence they come is a mystery*—and their velvet black wings, banded in metallic blue-green and flecked with red and gold, now radiate ever more brilliantly as the sunbeams glint off them, and, fluttering, by dozens, by hundreds, dizzy with the fragrance of the bloom, the glancing light sparkling from myriad refractions so bright one must almost shield the eyes, they engage in playful combats, dancing in their joyousness, crazy with delight, wheeling and soaring higher and higher above the tree, flying up and up till they are lost to sight.

The Xerces Blue
Glaucopsyche xerces

Amidst the scrub that grew on the dunes, like a momentary indecision of the plunging winds, flew the Xerces blue butterfly, a drunken king of motion unburdened by the world of desire.

As the fog came and went, the Xerces blue, with white spots on its dusty wings, fluttered about with the coastal green hairstreak, *Callophrys dumetorum*, and the two wavered carelessly like petals on the wind.

Now the wind buffets the houses, the coastal green hairstreak flies alone, and the Xerces blue, last seen near a pauper's cemetery, sleeps somewhere in the drowsy arm of stillness.

II.
Lost Animals
of Hawaii and
the Pacific Islands

"The Koa forests are almost all gone and those which remain will never again witness the scene once observed by Dean Amadon when the honeycreepers, 'high' on nectar, swarmed from treetop to ground level, vivid with different colors, 'constantly filtering' in excitement, calling, singing and 'whirring' like so many bright & fragile butterflies around a flowering tree in Eden."

– David Day, *The Doomsday Book of Animals*

With more than one hundred extinctions, the Hawaiian islands are commonly referred to as the extinction capital of the world. Not far behind is French Polynesia, with more than seventy.

The Black Mamo
Drepanis funerea

Deep in the tubes of the lobelia flowers hid the nectar perpetually sought by the black mamo, a honeycreeper, black from head to foot except for a small patch of yellow at the base of its absurdly long curved bill. After foraging from flower to flower, spending only a few seconds dipping in deep at each, rapidly darting their tongues in and out so they appeared like a liquid streak, their heads would emerge whimsically encrusted in pollen. Then they would sit quietly preening their feathers, stretching their necks this way and that to reach the fore parts of their bodies with their long bills, but never able to reach the tops of their heads.

Named 'funerea' for its somber plumage, the black mamo was tame and inquisitive, often approaching observers out of curiosity and perching overhead. Its song was a single long plaintive note. Only described on Moloka'i in 1893, the last one was shot in 1907. William Bryan is the last person known to have collected a specimen. Here is his first-hand account of that moment: "... litting from limb to limb scarcely stopping a second, eyeing me sharply all the while... Without further delay I availed myself of the first opportunity... and fired. The feathers flew."

The Greater Akialoa
Hemignathus ellisianus

The akialoas were a delight to behold. Olive-green with long, banana-shaped bills, they sang in short, soft trills as they darted from tree to tree, sipping the nectar of the lobelias—the *haha* and *oha-wai*—especially those with large corollas, sometimes stopping at the *ōhi'a lehua* or koa-tree flowers. They passed over and over the flowers, pausing for only a small taste before dashing hastily on to the next. They hopped along branches and scampered up trunks like woodpeckers. Carefree, perhaps swayed by the nectar, they sang joyously when not seeking food, in a scene of great merry-making, a scene now never to be repeated.

The Fanihi Flies at Night
Pteropus tokudae

Like miniature tropical superheroes, high in the branches of the tree canopy, the fanihi or Guam flying fox hung upside-down wrapped in their black capes with only their small furry-brown heads exposed. By day, they would sleep, or groom, or socialize with their neighbors. Often a male would entice a female to unfold her arms and soon the pair would wrap themselves up in inverted lovemaking. Then, when the light began to fade and it was time to forage for fruit, they would stretch out their long, membranous arms, let go of the branches and swoop out of the trees. With a couple of flaps of their great dark wings it seemed they alone could bring on the night.

The local Chamorro people long relished the fanihi as a delicacy for special occasions, so hunters climbed trees and swung large hoop nets to trap the foraging bats. When firearms were introduced, this manner of collecting gave way to predictably high yields. The fanihi was last seen in 1968.

Now night comes without the assistance of great dark wings.

The Hawaiian Rail
Porzana sandwichensis

A few hundred thousand years ago, the big island of Hawaii burbled up out of the sea. It was many years before plants and trees began to grow, but once they gained a foothold they transformed the island into a garden paradise. When the ancestors of the Hawaiian rail, perhaps blown off course in a storm while migrating, made this lucky landfall, they stayed. They shared the island with a few other birds, tree snails, spiders, bats and many insects.

When a genetic mutation caused the chicks to keep their infant-sized wings into adulthood, the Hawaiian rail, like many island birds, lost the power of flight. From then on, the rail scuttled about in scrub patches of forest along the slopes of the Kīlauea volcano. Hawaiians called it the *moho*, "bird that crows in the grass." They used its flightlessness to praise undaunted men in a proverb, *'A 'ohe mea nāna e ho 'opuhili, he moho no ka ta makani*, which means, roughly, "nothing can blow him off course, he is like a moho in the wind."

Preyed upon by introduced dogs, cats and rats, from which it could not fly away, the Hawaiian rail was last seen in the 1880s.

Last Song of the Laysan Honeycreeper
Himatione sanguinea freethii

For most of its life on this planet, no one was around to hear the Laysan honeycreeper sing. It lived on Laysan, a tiny but idyllic atoll flung in the middle of the Northwest Hawaiian Islands, where it flitted about in the scrub that surrounded the lagoon, feeding on insects and sucking honey from flowers with its down-curving bill. Of the many birds that called the island home, the Laysan honeycreeper was among the smallest.

When Walter Rothschild's collector Henry Palmer was on Laysan in 1891, he recorded this entry in his diary describing the bird's pluckiness:

> A most touching thing occurred. I caught a little red honeycreeper in the net, and when I took it out the little thing began to sing in my hand. I answered it with a whistle, which it returned and continued to do so for some minutes, not being in the least frightened.

If only this sort of unexpected and delightful communion was a reason why men explored distant islands in the first place.

Palmer described it as the rarest of the Laysan Island birds, though his diary reports that he saw "a fair number, generally in pairs."

Then came the feather collectors and guano miners, and the bird's fortunes soured. Rabbits were introduced and, being rabbits, they quickly multiplied and gnawed the island's vegetation down to the sand. By the time the scientists of the Tanager expedition arrived in 1923 to restore the island, so complete was the devastation that at first they spoke only in hushes; just three honeycreepers survived.

Expedition photographer Donald Dickey, who described the honeycreeper's song as "out of proportion to its size," sought to capture the bird on film. During a day of battling against wind and sun, Dickey chanced upon one of the three honeycreepers near the lagoon, "singing his heart out." His ten-second film clip shows a male honeycreeper perched on a rocky outcropping, bobbing its head up and down. Before the era of sound in film, the bird sings in silence.

Days later, a sandstorm engulfed the barren island and the remaining honeycreepers were swept away.

Dickey's last photo shows the bird in profile, its beak open, singing.

The Laysan Millerbird
Acrocephalus familiaris familiaris

The Laysan millerbird was small and drab, from the warbler family, which is known for its energetic and melodious singing. Visiting Laysan in 1913, ornithologist Alfred M. Bailey wrote of the birds' friendliness and curiosity:

> [they were] regular visitors to our table at mealtimes and to our workshops throughout the day, and so tame that if we remained quiet they would land upon our head. They searched in crannies for millers and caterpillars, their favorite food, and we often saw them over the portulaca flats bordering the lagoon. They were always extremely busy. It is probable that we were the last to see the species in life...

Later, when newly introduced rabbits denuded the island, three species of millers (moths) disappeared, and the familiar Laysan millerbird soon followed.

The Laysan Millers
Agrotis laysanensis, Laysan Noctuid Moth
A. procellaris, Procellaris Grotis Noctuid Moth
Hypena laysanensis, Laysan Dropseed Noctuid Moth

It's a hard beauty here: the roaring of the sea, the white sands, the pale green vegetation, all of it reminiscent of the magnificence of the desert. At sundown, the clouds radiate a splendor of golden violet or even greenish light before mellowing to darkness. Against the fading light and a backdrop of the steady rhythm of the surf, the cheerful calls of the never-roosting terns and the wailing moans of the shearwaters, the millers come out of their hiding places to follow the sweet aroma of the *pōhuehue* and *koali awa*, beach and blue morning glories, both in bloom.

There are nights when the sky is especially clear and striking, with the evening star bright enough to cast shadows and the white sand reflecting and magnifying the moonlight. Indeed, there are nights when the stars shine against the dark ground, and even the Milky Way becomes a lit-up cloud. Maybe tonight will be the night when the maiapilo blooms, and one could sense its intoxicating fragrance carried around the island by a wandering night breeze. Here, in this perfumed landscape, the millers fly about erratically in the night.

The Laysan Rail
Porzana palmeri

Flightless and fearless, the sandy-brown Laysan rail was swift and curious. It darted over the sand from one patch of grass to another or crept gingerly through the tall grass, poking its head around inquisitively. It was often seen stopped in the shade of a plant, one foot poised in air, peering at an object before advancing again in fits and starts. In spring, fuzzy-black chicks scuttled about under their parents, venting surprising amounts of noise.

In the only video of the Laysan rail, shot in 1923 by Donald Dickey, a bird scrambles from the bottom to the top of the frame with its head down, taking long, sure strides across the sand between a pair of coral outcroppings; an instant later, another dashes after it and for a moment it looks like a repeat of the same bird, running the same way. But then you see, just as the bird leaves the top of the frame, it flaps its short wings, once, twice, in an effort to catch its mate. If you loop this short clip, the chase goes on forever.

The Mamo
Drepanis pacifica

Prized for its golden thigh feathers which were used to make spectacular cloaks for Hawaiian royalty, little is known about this black and gold honeycreeper. In fact, ornithologists are only sure about a few things: it lived on the Big Island.

It loved to sip nectar with its long bill.

It was often seen in small groups, possibly families.

Its song was a single, long, mournful note.

It was last seen in 1898.

The Monarchs of French Polynesia
Pomarea pomarea (Maupiti)
P. nukuhibae (Nuku Hiva)
P. fluxa (Eiao)
P. mira (Ua Pou)
P. mendozae (Hiva Oa)

A volcano bursts through the ocean and creates an island. As the tectonic plates shift over the hotspot, the single island becomes a chain. The lava cools. Winds bring plants and insects. Trees grow. Before long, forests cover the mountain slopes and valleys. Birds that once flew over an empty patch of ocean now stop here to investigate. Other birds caught in storms find refuge here. Soon the monarch spends its days foraging in the understory for insects; males glossy black, females two-toned: black and white. In the morning, their flute-like melody floats through the trees.

By the time humans arrive, the forest is but a roadblock to development. And, after the rats arrive, the monarch goes silent.

The Oahu Tree Snails
Achatinella spp.

struck by a
raindrop snail
closes up
– Buson

Once you could shake an *ōhiʻa lehua* tree in the mountains of Hawaii and dozens of *kahuli* would come raining down. These "jewels of the forest"—tree snails—each had a colorful swirled shell as unique as a snowflake. They were striped and banded, brilliant red and smoky brown, metallic blue and electric yellow. Each one was like a craftsman's conical trinket polished to perfection.

But great beauty comes at a high price. They were collected by the thousands by Europeans. Hawaiians still pass down beautiful kahuli shell lei heirlooms. "Shell fever" decimated the numbers of snails. Later, the introduction of rats and the voracious wolf snail, together with rampant habitat destruction wiped out all but seven or eight of the original forty-two species of tree snails.

The few remaining snails spend most of their lives on a single ōhiʻa tree, eating the fungus that grows on the leaves. They have favorite hideouts, like under the small curl of a leaf or even between two leaves for protection. As hermaphrodites, the snails can impregnate each other. After coupling, each snail goes away pregnant; they give birth to live young one at a time.

Once they were thought to be the source of the singing in the trees that is now known to come from crickets. The snails sleep in the daytime, curled up in their colorful shells, and when the crickets begin singing, they go exploring.

The Song of the O'o
Moho braccatus

Once there was a love song that floated through the trees on the island of Kaua'i. All who heard the melody was smitten by its beauty. They said it was the sweetest song on the island, a few notes echoing early in the morning, like the sound of a flute, by turns melancholy and haunting. Who was the lover who sang such a song? When would the beloved respond? These were mysteries for the heart of hearts.

One day, some researchers walked into the forest with a recording of the song. They played it for the 'ōhi'a lehua trees with its succulent flowers and leathery leaves, thinking that was where the lover lived. Much as they hoped for an answer, none came. Today, the song of the ō'ō is heard no more.

The Shy Po'ouli
Melamprosops phaeosoma

Up in the dense mountainside rainforest of Maui, the last three black-faced honeycreepers lived isolated from one another, each within the boundaries of its own home range. Small, finch-like birds, the rarest in the world, they were too shy to have an actual song. Their quiet, infrequent *chits* were not loud enough to alert the others to their presence. They spent their time foraging or quietly perching in the *ohia*, *olapa*, and *ohelo* trees.

Perhaps they never knew of each other, or they didn't know what was at stake. Perhaps they knew they had no future. When a female was captured and brought to the male's home range, she stayed a few hours and flew home the next day, never once encountering her intended mate.

Soon after one of the birds was captured, it became ill, and the veterinarian felt pressure to save the bird and its species. But the bird died before a mate could be found, and the other two were never seen again. Now, perhaps in another mountain forest nearby, or perhaps far away on another island altogether, another species of bird is the rarest in the world.

The Tahitian Sandpiper
Prosobonia leucoptera

> The world is a mist. And the world is
> minute and vast and clear. The tide
> is higher or lower. He couldn't tell you which.
> His beak is focused. He is preoccupied
> looking for something, something, something
> – Elizabeth Bishop

Head down, beak poised, the white-winged Tahitian sandpiper foraged in a skiff of water along the highland river banks of Tahiti. If approached, it would scurry into the grass, whistling shrilly as it fled. Like sandpipers everywhere, the Tahitian sandpiper loved to run.

After Captain Cook's ships arrived with their rats and livestock, the Tahitian sandpiper ran into the mists and was never seen again.

Ula-ai-Hawane
Ciridops anna

Loulus—great fan palms—once dominated the lowlands of Hawaii, and a striking red honeycreeper used to eat its fruit. The ula-ai-hawane had a bright red body while its crown, breast, wing tips and tail were black and its head and neck were silver. It fed on the palm fruit, *hawane*, which earned it its name, "the red bird that feeds upon the hawane palm." This was likely its major food source. Sometimes it could be seen feeding with the equally showy black-and-gold mamo—together, the two colorful honeycreepers must have been a pretty sight.

Natives described the bird as "wild and shy, a great fighter... rarely taken by the hunter." When the rats arrived, they too fed on the palm fruit and seeds, and soon the great palm groves declined in number. In some places they vanished altogether. No one knows if the pugnacious ula-ai-hawane, whose song was never described, disappeared with or without a fight.

The Inquisitive Wake Island Rail
Gallirallus wakensis

"What you see is what you see," wrote Frank Stella of Minimalism in art. In his 1974 painting "The Wake Island Rail," one sees a gathering of French curves, partially overlapping; a lazy yellow swoop almost like a check mark; a blue note suggestive of a G-clef; a pair of railroad ties converging; a small red ornamental hook, hanging.

From the notes of ornithologist Charles Vaughn, who visited the island in 1938:

> They stand by dozens on the steps of the hotel kitchen door, peering thru the screen at the staff and going crazy with delight when one of the kitchen-boys comes out with scraps for them. They walk over his shoes and jump high in the air, just like young chickens at feeding time. During the heat of the day, they get under the hotel or go down into the rat burrows to keep cool; at night, they go foraging abroad with the rats.

What you don't see now you will never see again: flightless, grey-brown, with striking white bars on its flanks, alert and curious; poking out of cover with an erect head and a twitching tail; generally unafraid but ready to dart back into hiding at the slightest movement.

III.

Lost Animals of Central and South America

"'They are all beasts of burden in a sense,' Thoreau once remarked of animals, 'made to carry some portion of our thoughts.' Animals are the old language of the imagination; one of the ten thousand tragedies of their disappearance would be a silencing of this speech."

– Rebecca Solnit, *A Field Guide to Getting Lost*

Andean Black Toad
Atelopus ignescens

So strong is the mating urge. Down the hill they migrate, by the hundreds and for miles, black as shadows, risking death by crossing roads where so many are smashed. Onwards they go, towards a pond, a pool, standing water—a place to deposit eggs. They are slow, deliberate walkers, who will often stop, raise themselves up on their forelimbs, and scan around for other members of their species. He emits a low, chick-like peep, only heard nearby.

If he finds another male, he attempts to mount, but is soon repelled by slow kicks and soft peeps.

If he finds a pair in amplexus, he still tries to mount the male and receives a kick in the face that arcs him slowly onto his back. He struggles to right himself and, inevitably, if the couple has not escaped, tries again, with the same result.

If he finds a female, he mounts her, usually successfully, holds on and doesn't let go for days or weeks, until she deposits her eggs. Indeed, he hangs on as if his very life depends on it.

Basho and the Grebes
Podilymbus gigas, Atitlán grebe
Podiceps andinus, Colombian grebe

This is a story that ends prematurely. Once there was a diving bird that lived happily on a lake. This grebe, like grebes everywhere, had an elaborate mating ritual. Males and females faced each other, bobbed their long swan necks and preened their feathers in rhythm. They dove into the shallows, rose up breast to breast and, feet paddling furiously, waltzed around each other with their bills full of reeds as if proposing to build a floating nest together. Then, like fools in love, they dashed flirtatiously side by side across the surface of the lake before diving under.

* * *

The poet Bashō was fond of grebes. In "The Hut of the Phantom Dwelling," he relates a story of a monk who abandoned a hut near a mountain shrine, leaving it to be overgrown with brambles and bamboo grass, and ultimately for foxes and badgers to make their den there. After his long journey to the north, Bashō took up residence in the same hut, calling it home for several months. He cleared out the brambles, cut the grass, mended the thatch roof and patched the holes in the fence. He drew on the grebe for inspiration when he wrote to a friend,

> I am drifting by the waves of Lake Biwa. The grebe attaches its floating nest to a single strand of reed, counting on the reed to keep it from washing away in the current.

* * *

It is not known for how long Lake Atitlán, the volcanic lake in Guatemala, hosted the Atitlán grebe. Millennia, no doubt. A flightless waterbird, the Atitlán grebe fed on fish and crustaceans and nested among the reeds in the shallows of the lake. Locals called it the *poc*, after its mating call, a series of popping whoops followed by a more guttural, gulping sound.

* * *

> In the rain of the fifth month
> let us go and see
> the nest of the grebe.

Though Bashō is said to have remarked that he didn't like the diction of this poem, he liked the sense of going to see the nest of the grebe.

* * *

After his trip to the north, Bashō referred more frequently to his life in the sense of wandering or "floating." He incorporated the idea in his death poem:

> sick on my journey,
> only my dreams will wander
> these desolate moors

* * *

The Colombian grebe, which lived in the wetlands outside Bogotá, was described by locals as "confiding and easy to shoot while nesting." When disturbed, rather than hiding in the reeds, they swam out on open water. In the 1960s, entire colonies were shot to the last individual.

* * *

from all directions
winds bring petals of cherry
into the grebe lake

* * *

The Atitlán grebe suffered habitat loss as the locals cut the reeds to make baskets and mats. Shore front was cleared to build weekend chalets. Smallmouth and largemouth bass were introduced to the lake to attract sport-fishing tourists and the carnivorous fish ate the chicks. The lake became polluted from the increased population. The last two Atitlán grebes were seen on the lake in 1989 and after they died the species was declared extinct.

The Alaotra grebe was susceptible to an introduced carnivorous fish, the snakehead murrel, and entanglement in gillnets. It was declared extinct in 2010.

The Colombian grebe, in addition to hunting, suffered predation of its chicks from introduced rainbow trout, wetland drainage as its habitat was converted to agricultural land, pesticide pollution and reed harvesting. Last seen on Lake Tota in 1977, it was declared extinct in 1994.

* * *

hidden
in the winter waters:
a diving grebe

* * *

The flightless Junin grebe lives on Lake Junin in the highlands of west-central Peru. Declining water quality from nearby mining activities is endangering its long term prospects.

Sometimes on moonlit nights, the Atitlán grebe's distinctive mating call is said to be heard, *poc poc poc poc,* igniting rumors of its existence.

* * *

Bashō finishes his letter by saying, "Yet we all in the end live, do we not, in a phantom dwelling." Elsewhere he writes:

> the little grebe
> disappears... goes
> into the year end sea

The Chile Darwin Frog
Rhinoderma rufum

He blends into the forest floor like a dead leaf. He is immobile, and big as a thumbnail. When prey crawl too close, he strikes quickly with his sticky tongue. When threatened, he rolls over and plays dead. His world consists of a slow-moving stream in the forest, perhaps a bog. He likes to bask in the sun. After she lays eggs, he swallows them and incubates them in his vocal sac. Six weeks later, through one convulsion after another, he produces offspring from his mouth and they hop away. His call rings out like a tiny bell.

The Glaucous Macaw
Anodorhynchus glaucus

A shock of blue rising from the canopy flying against the sky, usually two—a long-formed bond—sometimes a group, their wings greenish-blue, their head and body azure—altogether glaucous—with a long tail as a sort of kite; their loud calls (*guaa guaa guaa!*) a raucous interruption to the river's lazy ride. Or, perhaps they sit, squawking on the branches crowning the banks, no squabble too small, cracking palm nuts and sharing the food, grooming their beautiful plumage.

Recalling the Golden Toad, Now Extinct
Incilius periglenes

Like a dream conjured by the pools of the cloud forest, longing for a splash of color amid the monotony of rot and decay far below the canopy. The pools themselves fleeting, brought by the mists that creep over the mountains of Monteverde, the spring rains. Neon Day-glo orange males, eyes like round black jewels, thought to be deaf and dumb, sensing by vibration, summoned from underground by the life-giving pools. And for a few weeks the pools became lively during the mating frenzy when the olive-colored females arrived. This went on once a year for a long time. The pools still awaken, but they can no longer summon the toads. Some dreams only come true once. On a night hike, flashlight beams shine into the clouds like searchlights in the cosmic dark.

The Extinction of the Falkland Islands Wolf
Dusicyon australis

A Tragedy in Five Acts

ACT I. The Falklands Islands wolf takes advantage of low sea levels and a narrow frozen marine strait during the last ice age to colonize the Falkland Islands, where it lives unmolested by other predators for thousands of years. It builds burrows and feeds on sea birds.

ACT II. The wolf is discovered by Captain John Strong when he lands on the islands in 1690. He compares it to a fox that is "twice as big as those in England." Seventy-five years later, in 1765, the wolf's curiosity is revealed when four of them run belly-deep into the sea to welcome a landing party from Commodore Byron of the HMS *Dolphin*. The sailors mistake the wolf's tame exuberance for ferocity and, unarmed, pull back to the ship.

ACT III. When Charles Darwin visits the islands on the *Beagle* in 1833-34, gauchos tell him they frequently kill the wolf by tempting it with a chunk of meat in one hand and then stabbing it with the other. Darwin describes the wolf's fearlessness: "They have been observed to enter a tent and actually pull some meat from beneath the head of a sleeping seaman."

Darwin sees the writing on the wall for the wolf. He writes: "Within a few years after these islands have become settled, in all probability this fox [wolf] will be classed as with the dodo, as an animal which has perished from the face of the earth."

Act IV. Not long after Darwin's departure, the colonial government sets a bounty on the animals. Hunters sent by fur dealer John Jacob Astor of New York beginning around 1839 fill his store with so many pelts the wolf is nearly extirpated.

Act V. The wolf is further demonized by Scottish settlers, arriving in the 1860s, for preying on cattle and sheep. Farmers lace dead geese with strychnine and place them in the wolf's burrows. Tales of wolves biting sheep in the neck lead to stories of vampires and the bounty is raised.

When the last one is shot in 1876, the Falkland Islands wolf entered the annals of extinction as the first canid to become extinct in modern times.

Rabb's Fringe-limbed Tree Frog
Ecnomiohyla rabborum

In the mountains of Panama, one could hear males calling for females throughout the year. If a call drew the wrong kind of attention, the frog could leap from the tree and use its large webbed hands and feet to glide safely to the ground.

Discovered in 2005, only a single male was heard, but not seen, calling in 2007 and silent ever since.

Said Joe Mendelson, the discoverer: "This one we caught just before it went off the planet."

A captive breeding program at Zoo Atlanta has failed.

The Red-bellied Gracile Mouse Opossum
Cryptonanus ignitus

Small enough to fit in the palm of your hand, mouse opossums had large black-marble eyes and a tail as long as their body.

The red-bellied gracile mouse opossum lived in the Andean highland forests of northern Argentina among rosewood, ceibil colorado and laurel trees. Since 1962, when this little-known and diminutive marsupial was first and last seen, most of the forest has been logged for cattle ranching and sugar cane, rendering our tiny friend homeless. Nothing is known of its preferences, habits or natural history.

Scrawny Stubfoot Toad
Atelopus longirostris

> Born out of a stone, he's living under a stone. He's building
> a tomb there.
> – Jules Renard, "The Toad," from *Nature Stories*

After its long, pointed snout, one next notices the yellow spots, standing out against the rust-purple colored, shagreened body.

Often he is out walking along the rocky streambeds among the lowland Andean evergreens, looking for a sunny patch. His reproductive habits are unknown. He sleeps on leaves close to the ground or hides under rocks.

Renard: *I often visit him, and each time I lift the stone up, I'm afraid of seeing him—and afraid he might not be there.*

Turquoise-throated Puffleg
Eriocnemis godini

> A heart the size of a pencil eraser, beating ten
> times a second, hammering faster than we could hear.
> – Luisa Ingloria, "Ode to the Heart Smaller than a Pencil Eraser"

In the north of Ecuador, below Colombia, in the ravines of Rio Guayllabamba, the turquoise-throated puffleg flits madly about as it seeks the red tubular flowers. Once found, it extends its long straw-like tongue and laps up the hidden nectar. The males show gold-green on top with hints of blue on their rumps, a turquoise love patch on their throats; the females less bright, more golden on their bellies, lacking the patch. Both feature snow-white downy leg puffs like frayed cotton balls or woolly panties. Living at altitudes of a few thousand meters, they dart aggressively from flower to flower to defend the high-energy nectar. Always on the verge of starvation, they kiss a thousand flowers a day. To survive the night, their hearts slow to tortoise speeds. Never abundant—one unconfirmed report from 1976—much of its habitat now erased. Once driving the diversification of ecosystems, the evolution of flowers, now in the past tense: its heart once hummed so strong.

The Twenty-Four Rayed Sunstar
Heliaster solaris

Shining on the sea floor like a dazzling yellow sun with twenty-four arms ablaze.

IV.
Lost Animals
of Europe

"Animals are our first memory," Werner Herzog says in *The Cave of Forgotten Dreams*, his film about the oldest human paintings, found in the Chauvet cave in southern France. In the film he tells a story. "In a forbidden recess of the cave, there's a footprint of an eight-year-old boy next to the footprint of a wolf. Did a hungry wolf stalk the boy? Or did they walk together as friends? Or were their tracks made thousands of years apart? We'll never know."

The Aurochs
Bos primigenius

Aurochsen blaze across the walls of caves in western Europe.

In the ancient epic of Gilgamesh, one is described as the Bull of Heaven: "And it came down from heaven snorting and bellowing. Euphrates shook. The city of Uruk shook and the Earth broke open under the great bull noise."

Their forms grace the Ishtar Gate of Babylon, alongside lions and dragons.

Julius Caesar described them in his account of the Gallic Wars as "a little below the elephant in size, and of the appearance, color and shape of a bull. Their strength and speed are extraordinary; they spare neither man nor wild beast which they have espied."

Known as the wild ancestor of modern cattle, the aurochs sought marshy forests and sedges and lost habitat as the European population grew, forcing them to compete for grass with domesticated cattle. As their numbers dwindled only the nobility had the privilege to hunt them. Though they formerly ranged across all of central Eurasia and northern Africa, by the 15th century, only a single population of aurochs remained in Poland.

The last aurochs died of natural causes in 1627.

Ivell's Sea Anemone
Edwardsia ivelli

Wary by nature, Ivell's sea anemone spends its time submerged in sediment on the bottom of Widewater Lagoon. Its long clear tentacles, ringed with cream-colored stripes, and splayed out like rays from the sun, blend into the sand and contract to catch unsuspecting prey. Preferring a sedentary life, sometimes it creeps slowly along the bottom in search of somewhere new, or inflates its tiny body and allows the current to carry it away.

The Madeiran Large White Butterfly
Pieris brassicae wollastoni

> This love letter, folded in two, is looking for a flowery address.
> – Jules Renard

The Madeiran large white flapped haphazardly through the ancient laurel forests of the Madeira islands, an archipelago north of the Canary Islands. Writing on air in big, loopy letters, it had a white body and large white wings with black tips. Fond of the north-facing valleys of the islands, with their abundant nectar-rich thistles and knapweeds, like other butterflies the Madeiran large white lives only for several weeks and males spend all their time seeking females to mate. While mating, they attach at the abdomen, as if folded in two. The Madeiran large white has not been seen since 1986.

Now no one receives its love letters.

Perrin's Cave Beetle
Siettitia balsetensis

> All knowledge is enveloped in darkness.
> – Thomas Browne

Instead of dipping a cup into the sea of forgetfulness to rescue a thought before it dissolves, or into the long and mysterious history of the Earth to quarry some unknown geological fact, Monsieur Sietti, the pharmacist of the French village of Beausset, was trying to quench his thirst from his well. To his surprise, when he pulled up the bucket, he discovered a previously unknown species of diving beetle.

A blind, marvelous fellow, its body a small oval with a helmet at one end, discolored from a life in darkness, its elongated legs fringed with bristles. The beetle was an excellent swimmer, actively paddling against the walls of the bucket. But, as if in protest for being lured from the shadowy depths, it only survived fifteen hours. Thought to live in the gravels of a submeander of the Var River, the beetle hasn't been seen in more than fifty years.

The Pyrenean Ibex, or Bucardo
Capra pyrenaica pyrenaica

> Ibexes (*ibices*) are like birds (*avices*) because they live in high
> places, so high that they are not visible to the human eye.
> – Isidore of Seville, *Etymologies*, seventh century

The wind rasps against the cliffs of Monte Perdido in the Maladeta Massif, itself risen from a tectonic collision millions of years ago. High in the thin air, eagles fly. Sometimes vultures circle too. Wallcreepers, their beaks curved like a curlew's, flit from one sun-baked rock to another. When they alight, they spread their brilliant crimson wings. Swifts dart from the overhangs and caves that look out onto the plunging valley, the vistas as grand as the silence.

In spring, the cliffs are fringed with icicles that can dangle fifty feet. Once loosened by the warming sun, their descendant whiz and crash could be heard for miles. To these lofty elevations came the bucardo, a wild goat whose males wore long, scimitar-like horns. After wintering in the lower valleys and grazing in snow-free meadows, where males fought furiously during the rut season, in April they returned to the higher elevations. With impressive agility, they would often pass along some narrow shelf where no man could follow, to seek out a hollow in the stone and lie down, rendering it invisible from above and below. On the scree slopes, the earth tones of its brown coat, flecked with black, allowed it to easily blend in, while in between, it browsed hidden in the dense undergrowth of scrubby beech and of box bushes ten feet high.

But the remoteness of the bucardo's habitat, combined with the male's thick, serrated, scimitar-like horns only added to its allure for trophy hunters. Legends sprang up about the healing powers of its body and drinking from its horn was said to protect one against poison. Hunters even had their tales, as Edward North Buxton, who later co-founded Flora and Fauna International, relates:

> Despair sometimes impels the ibex to face his rash pursuer on the
> edge of some pathless precipice, and he has been known to throw
> himself headlong onto the hunter, so that both have rolled over
> onto the abyss beneath, and miserably perished.

From the 1400s, when its population peaked, to the early 1900s, when it was finally protected, the bucardo suffered steady losses from hunting. The 20th century was no kinder, and the population dwindled from agricultural development, undernutrition due to competition with livestock and the chamois, another goat-antelope. In January 2000, Celia, the last Pyrenean ibex, was found crushed under a fallen tree—the first extinction of the new millennium.

Ironically, in the medieval version of the hunter's tale, the ibex escapes its pursuer by hurling itself down from the highest peaks, landing on its horns and lifting itself up unharmed.

The Sardinian Pika
Prolagus sardus

> When seen from a distance it looks like a small hare, but when captured it differs much from a hare both in appearance and taste. It lives for the most part under the ground.
> – Polybius, 3rd – 2nd century BCE

> My land is a stone of thirst and pain.
> – Ignacio Delogu, *My Land*, 1928

Buffeted by the bleak and bitter winds, the mountains jut out of the sea like icebergs, and spread their arms into craggy slopes that rumble down to the moors and the shore. Among the outcroppings on the moors, the pikas flee the perpetual sun and burrow underground. Sometimes they gather for grooming, sitting next to each other, combing their luxurious whiskers or rubbing their noses. Sometimes, when another intrudes upon the family group, a chase ensues. Through the heath and arbutus scrub, the twisted fig trees, guardians of time, tangle with the wild wind.

Ukrainian Migratory Lamprey
Eudontomyzon sp. nov. 'migratory'

Long had the lamprey swam the rivers: while the continents wandered, while the ice advanced and receded. Down to the sea to feed, up to the clear headwaters to spawn. Primitive, like a living fossil, a long wriggling pole with a toothed, funnel-mouth, they searched for the perfect place to build a nest, a small depression on the river bottom. Soon after laying and fertilizing thousands of eggs, the adults floated off to die. Once caught by fishermen for food, the lamprey has not been since the end of the 19th century.

V.

Lost Animals
of Australia and
New Zealand

"What is Missing?"

> – the title of artist Maya Lin's latest and last memorial,
> about the biodiversity crisis.

* * *

Between them, Australia and New Zealand are missing more than fifty species.

The Australian Hopping Mice
Notomys amplus, short-tailed hopping mouse
N. longicaudatus, long-tailed hopping mouse
N. macrotis, big-eared hopping mouse
N. mordax, Darling Downs hopping mouse
N. robustus, great hopping mouse

Once the sun goes down and the night rises, the hopping mouse pokes its nose out of its burrow and, with its beady eyes and big pink ears, surveys the surroundings. Much is to be feared in the dark. From above, an owl might appear. Now, foxes and cats prowl about. Suddenly, the mouse bound, hopping on its large hind feet like a tiny kangaroo. In fits and starts, darting from rock to hollow log, it nibbles on leaves, scavenges seeds and fruits. Moving quick, its long tail whips about behind. Later, when it is safe, it washes its face with its hands and grooms its brown coat.

The Sound of the Chatham Island Bellbird
Anthornis melanocephalus

Before the sky turned pink and my eyes would blink open, they, the *mako-makos,* gave a distinct and melodious singing, a tincture for the balm of the dawn. First one or two would ring, like tunable silver bells or ice clinking in fine crystal, then others would tink and tinkle, one by one, and link the din in a rolling melody that filled the valley. In the widening rink of light, in sync with the rising sun was once this drink of wild music.

* * *

On Captain Cook's voyage to Tahiti in 1770 to observe the transit of Venus, his naturalist Joseph Banks made these observations about the mako-mako or Chatham Island bellbird:

> I was awakened by the singing of birds ashore from whence we
> are distant not a quarter of a mile. Their numbers were certainly
> very great. They seemed to strain their throats with emulation and
> made perhaps the most melodious wild music I have ever heard,

almost imitating silver bells, but with the most tunable silver sound imaginable to which may be the distance was no small addition.

* * *

The sky blinking open singing the dawn bells of crystal clinking distant. Awake, straining the mako-mako shivers of ice ringing. In great numbers linked the light widening.

* * *

Cook himself described them similarly: "it seemed to be like small bells exquisitely tuned." Others reported regular concerts and the birds "gathering for the express purpose of singing together . . . each one contributing to the program." They sang duets against each other or solo to define territory. Young birds learned from their neighbors, so the tunes varied from place to place, like local dialects.

* * *

Before my eyes the sky a melodious balm: one or two, one by one rising.

* * *

Last sighted in 1906, the Chatham Island bellbird was driven to extinction by introduced cats and rats and forest destruction, as well as the activity of museum collectors.

* * *

A silver din, finely tuned.

* * *

The tink of time, wild.

Chatham Island Rails
Gallirallus modestus, Chatham Island rail
G. dieffenbachia, Dieffenbach's rail

> Islands are where species go to die.
>
> – David Quammen, *The Song of the Dodo*

Millennia ago, ancestors of the Chatham Island rail and Dieffenbach's rail descended from the South Pacific winds and settled on the Chatham Islands, a small archipelago some seven hundred kilometers southeast of New Zealand. With the lack of predators, the slow tinkering of natural selection allowed flightless descendents to survive and thrive. When humans brought their rats and cats, the adaptive traits became tragically maladaptive and these elegant ground-dwelling birds were quickly wiped out. The first European records of these birds were in the mid-to-late 19th century and the birds were gone before the century ended.

There are few eyewitness reports. Henry Travers, an amateur New Zealand naturalist, discovered the Chatham Island rail in 1872 on neighboring Manjare Island. He said it came out at dusk, evidently to feed on the sandhoppers near the beach. He found three of them "in a very rocky place and when disturbed sought to hide themselves among the stones." He caught the chick, whose plaintive cry attracted the mother, while the father escaped into the scrub.

Its feathers were a pale gray-brown and even the adult had a fluffy appearance, with some faint banding on its belly.

Ernst Dieffenbach, a German physician and naturalist, discovered the eponymous rail on a three-month visit to the islands in 1840. "I often heard its shrill cry in the bush," he said.

This cinnamon-colored rail, with dark brown barring on its back and white stripes on its belly, was larger than the Chatham rail and bore a gray streak above its eye.

By the time ornithologist Walter Buller visited the islands in 1855, none were found. He asked a native correspondent its status and was told, "If the bird still survives, I will catch you some. It was a beautiful bird. I remember seeing it when I was a boy."

The Mammals of Christmas Island
Rattus macleari, Maclear's rat
R. nativitatus, bulldog rat
Crocidura trichura, Christmas Island shrew
Pipistrellus murrayi, Christmas Island pipistrelle

> I hope there's an animal
> somewhere that nobody has ever seen
> And I hope nobody ever sees it.
>   – Wendell Berry's daughter, quoted in "To the Unseeable Animal"

For a long time, the fauna of Christmas Island went unseen. Only two hundred miles south of Java, the island, a raised coral atoll whose cliffs, rising up directly from the beach, may have resisted casual settlements. Still, it was close enough that the two species of rats and the shrew could have hitched a ride on tree rafts adrift on the Timor Sea. The two species of bats could have been swept there in a storm. Together, with many species of crabs and birds, they lived for thousands of years without any human interference.

There's some evidence that Polynesians came and went over the centuries but it wasn't until the late 1880s that Europeans set foot on the island and recorded their observations. According to Captain Aldrich, who spent ten days there in 1888, this was an island of crabs and rats. "When we first arrived," he wrote, "the huge crabs came about us in large numbers, in fact they swarm all over the island, so far as we saw it, and when halted for a few minutes one hears them approaching in all quarters."

Here, one would get the feeling of intruding on another's turf, no doubt. At dusk, the crabs disappeared into their burrows and were no longer seen or heard. Aldrich continues, "We were not without company, however, for the rats came out and were as abundant as the crabs." Naturalist C.W. Andrews, who visited in 1897 describes the scene: "Soon after sunset numbers may be seen running about in all directions and the whole forest is filled with its peculiar querulous squeaking and the noise of frequent fights."

The rats were devoid of fear. If a lantern was shone on them, they would approach it to investigate the new phenomenon. Andrews describes them as "a great nuisance, entering the tents or shelters, running over the sleepers, and upsetting everything in their search for food."

They were omnivorous and ravenous, eating everything from fruits high in the trees to shoes and boots carelessly left unattended. This was Maclear's rat, named for the captain of the *Flying Fish*, who brought back the first specimen in 1886. It had a grizzled, rufous brown appearance, with longer black hairs on its lower back, a light belly, and a tail as long as its body.

* * *

While Maclear's rat swarmed everywhere, the bulldog rat was much less widespread, preferring the hilly areas of the interior. Stouter, with a thick layer of fat on its back, and a small and delicate head, it was a dark umber brown all over and had long, thick, coarse fur. Andrews noted they lived in small colonies in burrows, among the roots of a tree. Often several were found living in the long, hollow truck of a fallen, half-decayed sago palm. Like Maclear's rat, they ate fruits and young shoots, and even the bark of some trees.

They never climbed trees, and they stayed hidden in their burrows until dark. When exposed to direct sunlight, they would become dazed.

* * *

The fortunes of the rats changed rapidly. By 1899, a phosphate mining company was set up, beginning an epoch of woe for scores of indentured laborers, and in 1908, Andrews returned to see how the settlement affected the rats.

"In spite of continual search," he wrote, "not a single specimen of either species could be found in any part of the island."

With the mining operation, more ships were coming and going and sometime between 1901 and 1904, black rats (*Rattus rattus*), who wreaked so much havoc on the bird populations of other islands, invaded the island. Some were infected with trypanosome and the disease quickly spread to the resident species, and, without immunity, they were wiped out.

Andrews is also responsible for much of what we know about the resident shrew. It had a long snout, dark gray fur and poor eyesight, so it relied on its other senses to probe among the leaf litter of the rainforest on the plateau and adjacent to the shoreline for beetles. He writes, "This little animal is extremely common all over the island and at night its shrill squeak, like the cry of a bat, can be heard on all sides."

But the population suffered a large crash at the same time as the rats. When he returned in 1908, he wrote, "The shrew is probably extinct, at least no specimen was either seen or heard during my visit."

In fact, the shrew survived and two were seen both in 1958 and 1985, but none have been seen since.

* * *

The Christmas Island pipistrelle was the island's smallest mammal, weighing less than a nickel, and is thought to have played a role in the island's ecosystem for about a million years. It had brown fur and big ears, and fed on moths, beetles and flying ants. When the population was healthy, they roosted on tree hollows in groups of fifty or more but after the decline in the mid-1980s, the last colony of twenty all roosted under one piece of bark in the same tree. Males aren't part of the colonies and tend to roost individually.

Females produced one pup per year and left them alone at night while out to feed, exposing the young to a variety of nocturnal predators. They were weak flyers that fluttered like butterflies. They typically lived four to five years.

The last one was seen in late August, 2009, flying near the refugee detention camp. Tim Flannery speculates on what happened to it:

> Perhaps it landed on a leaf at dawn after a night feeding on moths and mosquitoes, and was torn to pieces by fire ants; perhaps it succumbed to a mounting toxic burden placed on its tiny body by insecticide spraying. Or maybe it was simply worn out with age and ceaseless activity, and died quietly in its tree hollow.

A photo shows one of the last pipistrelles clinging to the tip of a human finger.

Desert Rat-Kangaroo
Caloprymnus campestris

Here, gone; here again, gone again.

Almost a century between sightings.

A legendary runner, once chased for twelve miles across the hard-packed gibber plains in the heart of Australia. Barely seen in the distance where *seeming scarcely to touch upon the ground, it almost floated ahead in an eerie, effortless way.* Easily tiring a relay of three galloping horses. *Its speed, for such an atom, was wonderful, and its endurance amazing.*

'*Caloprymnus*' for "beautiful rump," alluding to the exquisite shape of its powerful hind legs; and '*campestris*', to its habitat, "plain, level country," altogether less musical than the Aboriginal: *oolacunta*.

Sometimes known as the buff-nosed rat-kangaroo, the oolacunta was the size of a small rabbit, had a small muzzle, narrow ears and sandy brown fur that blended into the clay soils. They built flimsy nests of leaves and grasses, carrying materials with their prehensile tails, and hid under its twigged roof during the heat of the day, emerging at night to feed.

Sometimes you could see one peeking out the top. When danger pressed, it escaped out the side door and ran for its life, hopping with an easy stride, trunk leaned well forward and tail almost straight, so light on the ground it didn't kick up any dust.

The Gastric-brooding Frog
Rheobatrachus silus and R. vitellinus

The gastric-brooding frog mother always knew where her babies were: inside her. After the male fertilized the eggs, she would gather them in her mouth and swallow them whole. The eggs were surrounded by a jelly with a substance that stopped the production of hydrochloric acid in her stomach so that they weren't digested. When they hatched, the tadpoles secreted this same substance.

Not much larger than a human thumb, the female grew larger and larger as the tadpoles developed inside her. During the six weeks of incubation, she did not eat, though she remained active. When ready, she would burp out as many as two dozen fully formed juveniles one at a time.

The two known species were predominantly aquatic and had small geographic ranges in eastern Australia. The southern species (*R. silus*) was discovered in 1972 and last seen in 1981. The northern species (*R. vitellinus*) was discovered in Eungella National Park in 1984 and disappeared the next year.

Greater Short-tailed Bat
Mystacina robusta

> A shred of night creeps into every single corner.
> – Jules Renard, "Bats," *Nature Stories*

All over the world as dusk deepens into night, bats take wing out of their darkened roosts to search for food. In New Zealand, short-tailed bats crawl out of their burrows and forage on the forest floor as eager as a mouse. With their wings tucked into a pouch and using their arms as legs, they run through the leaf litter, rooting out worms and insects, like their ancient shrew-like ancestors. Sometimes they fossick in groups, even if they are poor at sharing the spoils. Sometimes they scurry up trees and along branches, and prey upon chicks in nests.

When they fly, they fly low, making their signature erratic turns, perhaps to swoop down onto a flower and sip its nectar.

In late summer, males gather in leks and croon for the attention of females.

Always there is the danger of the laughing owl, who watches and waits to pounce.

The Huia
Heteralocha acutirostris

In the early dawn of the land of the long white cloud, the clear, flute-like song of the huia rang out, penetrating the dense forest and could be heard a great distance away: *uia, uia, uia,* as if to ask, *where are you?* though the mates were never far apart. Such graceful birds, with their black plumage and luster of blue-green iridescence, a white band on the tip of their much-desired tail feathers, their ivory bills a striking contrast: his a straight, stout chisel, hers a long delicate curve, like a honeycreeper's.

Together they hopped from branch to branch, slightly opening their wings, flying only short intervals and resting a moment to spread the tail into a broad fan, sometimes consorting with another pair that made up a small party of delight. They stayed in the shade, in the thick of the moist forest laden with mosses and ferns and often would find a rotted log or branch and he would attack it with gusto, sending a spray of bark everywhere and she with her slender bill would follow to delicately pluck out the huhu larvae but not share it.

Later, one could see them coming back together to caress each other with their ivory bills, uttering at the same time a low affectionate twitter before bounding off, flying and leaping in succession to some favorite feeding place far away to the silent depths of the forest.

The Laughing Owl, or Whekau
Sceloglaux albifacies albifacies and S. a. rubifacies

When it flies, the whekau laughs. Just before the rain, the whekau hoots a melancholy note. On dark and drizzly nights, the whekau loudly cries a series of dismal shrieks. For no good reason, the whekau chuckles like a turkey, mews or yelps like a cat or dog. Whenever it feels like it, the whekau whistles absolutely tunelessly.

The Lesser Bilby
Macrotis leucura

The bilby lived in the harsh desert of central Australia and only came out at night. During the day, he hid deep in its spiral burrow and slept in a sitting position: squatting on its hind legs, he tucked in its long muzzle, folded his long rabbit-like ears over his eyes, and sank into sleep.

Unlike the docile greater bilby, the lesser bilby was ill-tempered, "fierce and intractable, and repulsed the most tactful attempts to handle them by repeated savage snapping bites and harsh hissing sounds." He grew to rabbit size and was hunted for its smooth, silky fur.

Widely dispersed and never abundant, on nights of strong winds, heavy rains or a full moon, the lesser bilby stayed hidden in its burrow.

The Pig-footed Bandicoot
Chaeropus ecaudatus

> And Karora was thinking, and wishes and desires flashed through his mind. Bandicoots began to spring from his navel and from his armpits. They burst through the sod above, and sprang into life.
> – Arrernte creation story

They spread out into the parched country of the sand plains and sand dunes with its spinifex and tussock grass, its mulga overstorey, into the open woodlands where they scraped out some soil to build a nest lined with dry grass or dug a shallow burrow. It was good land, some said— good for nothing. "A bandicoot would starve on it."

So the plump-bodied pig-footed bandicoot, with its spindly legs and delicate hoof-like feet, such a dainty marsupial, orange-brown above and fawn below, with long pointed ears (but shorter than the ears of bilbies), and a long, pointed snout, ate meagerly of the grasses and insects, hopping about like a rabbit and transforming an awkward, quadrupedal run into a smooth gallop at great speeds when necessary.

After the young were born and nursed in the pouch, they left the pouch and followed the mother in forays for food, seeking sustenance in the warm evening sun.

The Thylacine on YouTube
Thylacinus cynocephalus

Have you seen the video of the last thylacine? It paces around in its cage, yawns and displays its formidable jaws, its incredible teeth. They called it the Tasmanian tiger because of the stripes blazed across its back, rump and the base of its tail, though it looks like a wild dog and has a kangaroo's stiff tail. It sniffs the air, lies in the sun, crouches like a raccoon, gnarls a meaty bone, paces round and round as if it has nothing better to do, as if it has all the time in the world.

The Toolache Wallaby
Macropus greyi

At dusk, the toolache wallabies gathered in mobs in the swampy grasslands of South Australia. After resting in the shade all day, now they groom, play box and inevitably, the males fight for the right to mate.

If they were prone to vanity, they would show off their beautiful coats to one another, ashy brown and tinted yellow, with black-tipped ears and a yellow streak on their cheeks, all the rage in Melbourne and Sydney.

When chased, they were nonchalant, letting the dogs come close, then bounding away like an antelope with first a short jump, then a long one, leaving the dogs far behind.

VI.
Lost Animals
of Asia

"Our findings suggest that as soon as even 'megafaunal' species stop being encountered on a fairly regular basis, they immediately start to become forgotten. They are truly 'out of sight, out of mind.'"

– Dr. Samuel Turvey, on the rapid disappearance of local knowledge about even distinctive animals like the baiji and Chinese paddlefish.

The Baiji, Goddess of the River
Lipotes vexillifer

Once there was a princess who lived on a tall sailing ship on the Yangtze River. She had a carefree life and spent her days swimming in the currents of the river, collecting shells, strolling along the lush river banks. Her father, the Emperor, thought she was wasting her life and arranged for her to marry a wealthy prince. Seeing how her life would change and knowing that she did not love the man, the princess refused. When she told her father he flew into a rage. Blind to her desires and unwilling to allow shame to be brought upon the family for such impiety, he drowned her in the river. But the river took pity on her and turned her into a dolphin. She became known as the baiji, the Goddess of the River.

* * *

The baiji had a long upturned beak that gave it the appearance of perpetually smiling. It liked to swim in eddy counter-currents and communicated by clicks and whistles. Functionally blind, the baiji navigated the murky water with sonar for twenty million years. But as the local population grew, the baiji's sonar was easily disrupted by the heavy motorized boat traffic. It got caught in fishing nets, on rolling hooks, by electrical charges, in the never-ending river development projects.

Last minute efforts to relocate the baiji failed and none have been seen since 2004. Like the princess who was looking for love, the baiji wasn't loved enough to be saved.

The Chinese Paddlefish
Anodorhynchus glaucus

In the sky above the long river, the moon comes and goes. From the trees, the gibbons call. Echoing through the gorges, the temple bell is heard. Up and down the river swims

the paddlefish, sometimes skimming below the surface, sometimes cruising deeper. Mouth agape under its protruding spoon-bill snout, it feeds on zooplankton, answers an ancient urge to swim up through the gorges—where the clouds often creep low—and spawn upriver. Down to the sea swim the juveniles. Oh, the once wild river. On the shores, the fishermen put out their lamps, haul in their boats, sing their drunken goodbyes and marvel at the changed world. Like a lone gull between the heavens and the earth, the moon drifts on the great river.

The Demise of the Javan Tiger
Panthera tigris sondaica

As a child Jorge Luis Borges used to linger before the tiger cage at the zoo. He liked its natural beauty, its physicality, its black and gold stripes. He drew pictures of tigers and judged books of natural history "by the splendor of their tigers." They later prowled wordlessly through his stories and poems.

As an adult, he yearned to dream of tigers but lamented, "Never can my dreams engender the wild beast I long for." Though the tiger appeared, it was always a poor replica, too flimsy, the wrong size or shape, or all too fleeting, as if it had somewhere better to be.

* * *

William Blake's poem about the tiger, described as the most anthologized poem in English, doesn't once mention the characteristic stripes we all love. Instead, Blake admires the tiger's "fearful symmetry," as if the stripes were a sort of existential frame that the animal inhabited after some rite of passage.

* * *

Blind, Borges woke from his dreams in a sweat because he could no longer properly visualize a tiger.

* * *

A black and white photo of a Bali tiger, taken in 1925, shows it hanging upside-down, its paws tied to a thick pole carried by several village men. One man holds the tiger's tail; another stands behind the tiger, still sporting his hunting jacket and cap. The last Bali tiger was shot in 1937.

Though the Caspian tiger was thought to be extinct since the 1950s, it is now known to be genetically similar to the Siberian tiger, of which less than 400 adults remain. Yet this population suffers from extremely low genetic diversity, and extinction remains a threat. Most other tiger species have at most several hundred adults, except the Bengal tiger, which has almost 2500 adults. In 1900, there were about 100,000 tigers in the world, and now there are perhaps 4000. The Javan tiger was last seen in the mid-1970s.

* * *

One of Borges' poems begins: *I imagine a tiger.*

* * *

In the famous tale "The Lady, or the Tiger," a young man is punished by a "semi-barbaric" king for loving his daughter, the princess. The young man is forced to choose between two doors, behind which are either a ferocious tiger, or a lovely maiden who will marry the young man. Either way, the young man will no longer trouble the king. Before the judgment, the princess lies awake nights, by turns fearful for her lover's life and jealous of losing him to a rival beauty. On the day of the judgment, she finds out what is behind each door and secretly signals which door to select. He chooses accordingly, and the author leaves us with the question: Which came out of the opened door—the lady, or the tiger?

In a modern version of the tale, a tiger still paces behind one of the doors, and behind the other door there is nothing. Nor is there a king or a princess. There is only us, so jealous of the tiger's land, so eager to profit. So the question remains: who will help us choose the right door?

* * *

One of the questions in Yann Martel's *Life of Pi* is whether the Bengal tiger, who goes by the name of Richard Parker, is real or imagined. Despite spending 227 days on a lifeboat with the protagonist, Pi Patel, being kept alive by him and in turn provoking him to survive, when the boat strikes land in Mexico, Richard Parker bounds out and, perhaps ready to live his own story, disappears into the jungle without looking back.

* * *

Like Borges, I have trouble imagining a tiger. When I try, I usually conjure a circus performer jumping through a burning hoop instead of one of nature's greatest hunters. If I keep trying, I can summon up an image of a tiger lying around bored in a zoo. Before long, that image is replaced by Rilke's panther, pacing back and forth as if behind a thousand bars, and beyond these bars no world. At times, the panther opens its eyes to let in an image of utter stillness, but it soon vanishes.

* * *

Walking on the outskirts of Buenos Aires as the sun went down, Borges and a friend quoted another poet to each other: "Let the eternal sun die like a tiger."

Ilin Island Cloudrunner
Crateromys paulus

Imagine the Ilin Island cloudrunner creeping among the branches of the pine and oak trees that used to grow among the clouds of its island home, its padded feet adapted to arboreal life, flicking its bushy tricolored tail, stopping now and then to gather fruit and leaves in its large fore claws, sitting upright to eat and, oblivious to any consequent danger, chewing its food loudly.

The Japanese River Otter
Lutra lutra whiteleyi, later L. nippon

In the country of rich reed beds, on the island of many dragonflies, otters romped on the banks of the rivers like children at play. How many there were no one knew. Their dark brown coats slick with wetness, a long thick serpentine tail, they were part of the rivers, like the herons and egrets, swimming with their noses in the air, eyes squinting, chasing each other in made-up games of tag and hide 'n seek on the banks and in the water, wrestling. When they were hungry they plunged into the water and came up with a fish that they ate greedily, leaving the remains on the banks like a sacrifice for the gods. Lithe and palpable in the pool of the moment, the water didn't splash when they dove in.

The Japanese Sea Lion
Zalophus japonicus

On the coasts and islands of northeastern Asia, around the Sea of Japan, the Kuril Islands to the southern tip of the Kamchatka Peninsula lived the Japanese sea lion, as at home in the sea, speeding through the water like an agile torpedo, as hauled out on open sandy beaches sunning themselves in boisterous colonies of fifty or more. Sometimes they sheltered in island caves that resounded with a perpetual bellowing of the bulls asserting themselves before their aggregate of cows, and the cows calling for their pups after a spell of feeding. Known to be playful, young sea lions played "King of the Castle" and defended the right to stand atop a boulder, pushing aside all challengers. Or they made games with giant pieces of kelp, shaking and tossing them about. Older males would daringly slip in among the cows and mate with one until barked away by the dominant bull.

Hunted for their oil, their last home was on the volcanic Liancourt Rocks, site of a territorial dispute between Japan and South Korea, when fifty to sixty were seen in 1951.

Ridley's Stick Insect
Pseudobactricia ridleyi

Within "the countless tribes of interesting insects" hidden in the virgin forest of Singapore, Ridley's stick insect was ponderously slow, as if the branches themselves were learning to walk. Easily disguised at the best of times, when the forest was cleared it disappeared.

Schomburgk's Deer
Rucervus schomburgki

> Outside space and time, the deer wander, at once swift and languid.
> – Juan José Arreola

During the day, the small herds rest with their young in the shade, during the evening, they move about like apparitions in the swampy plains of the Chao Phraya River Valley. They graze the grasses, slip among the thickets, invisible in their chocolate brown coats. The male's antler's curl forward, all the main tines branching into a sort of basket. Immobile or mobile, they move timelessly through time, as if out of a grove in a legend. They run without effort. They stop and something remains outside them, galloping.

The Shrub Frogs of Sri Lanka

> The sun touched you
> once in that forest. You glowed,
> then you were gone.
> – Zilka Joseph, *The Kenyon Review*, 2012

> The ubiquitous tinkling calls of the shrub frogs of the genus
> Philautus help to characterize the forests of tropical Asia.
> – Meegaskumbura et al., *Zootaxa*, 2007

Around Sri Lanka's central mountains and in the "wet zone," before the tea and rubber plantations, before the cinchona and coffee plantations, trees populated the slopes of the mountains and gathered in rain forests. In these forests were twenty-one species of frogs who are only known today from specimens collected in the last century, often more than one hundred years ago. Once they sang in the forests, by day and night, touched by the sun and rain, now they are mute in jars in museums. Among them—

one, *Adenomus kandianus*, was named after Kandy, the ancient city in the highlands;

one, *Nannophrys guentheri*, was named after zoologist Albert Gunther, whose descriptions of thousands of species influenced the work of Darwin and Wallace;

one, *Philautus dimbullae*, was named for the tea growing region;

one, *P. eximius*, for its strikingly unusual pale-yellow coloring;

one, *P. extirpo*, for being already extinct;

one, *P. malcolmsmithi*, for herpetologist Malcolm Smith, both a field naturalist and museum man;

one, *P. nanus*, for being small;

two, *P. nasutus* and *P. oxyrhynchus*, for their sharp or pointed snouts;

one, *P. pardus,* for its leopard-like spots;

one, *P. maia*, from the Greek word for 'good mother', as she was found protecting a clutch of eggs under her stomach;

one, *P. rugatus*, for its wrinkled skin;

and one, *P. zal*, named (according to its discoverers) as a way "to express our sadness and frustration at the loss of so many Sri Lankan amphibians."

The Polish word *zal* means a sadness or regret, a burning hurt, like a howling inside you that is so unbearable that it breaks your heart.

Spectacled Cormorant
Phalacrocrorax perspicicillatus

On the rocky coasts of the islands at the western end of the Aleut chain lived the largest of the cormorants. Black with steel-blue reflections on its neck and a yellow ring around the eyes, giving the bird its name, the spectacled cormorant was described by Georg Steller, the only naturalist who saw it, as large, clumsy on land and almost flightless. Beyond that, almost nothing is known of the bird.

A quote from Steller tells us how the cormorant fared upon meeting shipwrecked sailors:

> They weighed 12-14 pounds so that one single bird was sufficient for three starving men.

Discovered in 1741 and last seen in the 1850s, after the islands were plundered by whalers, fur traders and hunters, only Stellers' records and a handful of specimens tell us the bird ever existed.

Steller's Sea Cow
Hydrodamalis gigas

Strange to come upon them quietly gathered in the bay, their massive black backs humped above the water as they fed on the seaweed below, the silence broken only when one raised its head and deeply drew in a breath of air. As large as elephants, submerged, with gulls perched on their backs, the sea cows ate their fill of kelp and rolled over to take a nap, careful to move away from the shore so as not to be left on dry land by the outgoing tide. None were heard to snore, which, given their enormous size, would have been a formidable sound. The only other sound that was heard were the moans of the wounded, who thrashed about trying to free themselves from the harpoon, breathing heavily, as if sighing.

* * *

One needs only to read this small excerpt from explorer George Steller's 1751 account, *De Bestiis Marinis*, "The Beasts of the Sea," to know that something incredibly precious has been lost with the extinction of Steller's sea cow due to overhunting:

> But if one animal is caught with the hook and begins to plunge about rather violently those near him in the herd are thrown into commotion as well and endeavor to assist him. To this end some of them try to upset the boat with their backs, others bear down upon the rope and try to break it, or endeavor to extract the hook from the back of their wounded companion with a blow from their tails, and several times they proved successful. It is a very curious evidence of their nature and of their conjugal affection that when a female was caught the male, after trying with all his strength, but in vain, to free his captured mate, would follow her quite to the shore, even though we struck him many blows, and that when she was dead he would sometimes come up to her as unexpectedly and as swiftly as an arrow. When we came the next day, early in the morning, to cut up the flesh and take it home, we found the male still waiting near his mate…

Yunnan Lake Newt
Cynops wolterstorffi

Until the 1950s, you could find the Yunnan lake newt swimming in the shallows of Kunming Lake, the "Sparkling Pearl Embedded in the Highlands" of Yunnan. Whether lurking among the aquatic plants along the lakeshore, hiding in nearby ponds and marshes, the Yunnan lake newt lived a life of secrets. Black with a blaze of orange down its spine and orange spots on its body, the male's tails turned deep blue during mating season when they were found by the thousands congregating around the reeds and lillies at the lakeshore, searching for mates. If he was lucky, she would respond to his "tail-fanning" display and receive him.

In winter, they disappeared into the depths of the lake to hibernate.

Last seen in 1979, the Yunnan lake newt suffered from the growth of the nearby city of Kunming and the increase of industrial waste and domestic sewage, which was dumped directly into the lake, destroying its habitat.

VII.
Lost Animals
of Africa

"I am the animal and the animal is me."

– African proverb

The Bluebuck
Hippotragus leucophaeus

Apart from his harem, the bull antelope stands erect, the curve of his ringed horns sweeping back behind his head as if defining an equation of perfection, ending in points sharp enough to slice the wind. His coat, a hunter's prize, glows faintly like the blue sky. He and the small herd rest in the heat of the day and late in the afternoon they graze in the grassy valleys, the savannahs on the tip of the continent. The bull stays vigilant and watchful.

When another bull approaches, he arches his neck, holds his head high, turns his ears sideways. If the intruder doesn't lower his head, wave and tuck in his tail, they will clash horns and head butt. His call is a blowing snort.

The Meek Bubal Hartebeest
Alcelaphus buselaphus buselaphus

Though the bubal hartebeest carried its huge beam head as stylishly as possible, its melancholy eyes, humped shoulders, sloping quarters and particularly its long, long face gave the antelope a deprecatory appearance, as if it apologized for its very existence. Meekness was its virtue. Its small horns strikingly outlined the shape of a lyre though from the side their lazy curves made it seem like a pair of egrets had taken root and spent their time gazing hopelessly skyward.

The bubal hartebeest moved at a smooth and swinging canter, flicking its rear legs fleetly as it ran with great endurance over the lowland mountains of northern Africa. Chased, it easily fled its pursuers and, perhaps contrite, would often stop and stare its foe full in the face with a most humble look, as if it didn't mean to escape, as if it couldn't help itself. Then, with a violent sneeze, once more it would bolt ahead.

The Cape Verde Giant Skink
Macroscincus coctei

> In the parched path
> I have seen the good lizard
> (one drop of crocodile)
> meditating.
>   – Federico García Lorca, "The Old Lizard"

Like an old Zen monk, his fat body immobile (a tail of stillness), he watches the sun smoulder in the sky, smiling his placid smile, the land parched behind him.

It rains sometimes in the fall (two drops of desert) and he searches for food in the burrows, among the bushes, before the island withers (an egg, a chick, a few seeds, something green), sniffing the air with his tongue. He thrives on the cusp of oblivion (shoemakers, hunters, convicts, the inevitable droughts and avid museum collectors) while the ocean surges below.

The sun rises, the sun dissolves; he gazes into the broken horizon. Exiled on this pile of rocks, he is a king without a country, a serpent out of time (a koan of nonbeing).

The Ethiopian Water Mouse
Nilopegamys plumbeus

In a stream that becomes a river that becomes the Nile, a mouse swims in search of its dinner. Nose parting the water, hind feet paddling madly, he stops to rest on an island—scarcely more than a rock with a few tufts of grass—his slate-colored coat matted so thick he has no need of shivering. He sniffs the air, smooths his dripping whiskers, looks about. Long had his kin thrived in the highlands, below the huddling acacia and shrubbery that crowd the banks, finding their own paths through the grass to the water. This was not so long ago, before the land was shorn, before the water took back what the water once gave.

Lake Alaotra Grebe
Tachybaptus rufolavatus

With its short wings, the Alaotra grebe could not fly long distances and had no other home but Madagascar's Lake Alaotra, shallow, reed-fringed. In the only known photo of the Alaotra grebe, the black-capped bird paddles alone on the water. Against a backdrop of reeds, it swims among the shadows, leaving a small wake.

Lake Pedder Earthworm
Hypolimnus pedderensis

From Jules Renard's *Nature Stories*: "You can see one there, lying down, stretched out like a lovely noodle."

On a beach of the lake, before it was flooded.

Lake Victoria Cichlids
Haplochromis spp.

In the middle of the East African Rift Valley, between the Serengeti Plains and the Mountains of the Moon, not far from the tree where man was born, sprawls Lake Victoria. One could call it the lake of many names for it is also known as Victoria Nyanza, Nalubaale, Ukerewe, Sango, Lolwe and the Eye of the Rhino. It straddles the equator and is the source of the Nile River. Though the lake is only four hundred thousand years old and it dried out during the last glacial maximum fourteen thousand years ago, it has become the home of some five hundred species of cichlid fish, one of the great biological radiations in history.

As the basin dried out with the Ice Age, a few cichlid species sought refuge in the rivers flowing into the lake, waited out the long period of dryness, and then repopulated the lake when the waters returned. New niches were available to be occupied, from deep water habitat to places around the rocky islands and marshy coastline. Soon the founding species diversified into hundreds of unique and colorful species.

While other fish lay thousands of eggs and let the hatchlings fend for themselves, cichlids protect their fry from predators by carrying them—

often several dozen—in their mouths. The parent can graze algae and nourish their young at the same time. Smaller populations allowed mutations to spread more quickly, possibly contributing to the diversification of the species.

Despite being an evolutionary phenomenon, the cichlids have suffered as the fishing industry has expanded. Around 1900, British colonial officials introduced gill nets, which greatly increased catches. With greater fish catches, more people settled by the lake and began clearing land for agriculture. Frequent rains brought soil and fertilizer into the lake in runoff. Fertilizer caused algal blooms on the lake surface and when they died they sank to the bottom and decomposed, absorbing oxygen required by the fish at deeper lake levels.

Overfishing soon led to declining fish yields and to remedy this, in 1954 the British officials introduced the Nile perch, a huge predatory fish that would support a new fishery and attract sport fishermen. The Nile perch population thrived by preying on the cichlids, which were soon decimated. Perhaps two hundred species of cichlids have become extinct in one of the worst vertebrate mass extinctions of modern times.

Ironically, around the lake the Nile perch as nicknamed *mkombozi*, "savior" in Kiswahili, for its enormous effect on the local economy. Yet it too is being overfished and the algae blooms are killing the lake.

Miss Waldron's Red Colobus Monkey
Piliocolobus badius waldronae

When the monkey dies his cheeks are full of laughter. Two rows of bared white teeth. Always smiling. You could hear him calling to others in the treetops. Chattering and shrieking. Never quiet. He hides his fear with nervous prattle. Deep-set eyes, a face of mischief never photographed, he is a mystery to himself. His tail sweeps the air. When the hunter comes he flees to the highest branches to join the others like a troop of fools, chattering and shrieking. Too beautiful to live. Death always stalks him. Too beautiful to survive. Death always follows him.

(after the Yoruba hunter poems)

The Wandering Rhino
Diceros bicornis longipes, western black rhinoceros

One of the earliest Buddhist texts, from the first century, is known as the Rhinoceros Sutra because of its refrain. In a series of verses, it cautions against community life and companionship, and admonishes seekers to "wander alone like a rhinoceros."

One of the verses reads, "Doing no violence to living things, not even a single one of them, wander alone like a rhinoceros."

And another, "Seek a solitary dwelling like a lion, the forceful, fanged, conquering king of beasts, and wander alone like a rhinoceros."

* * *

Most species of rhinos are solitary and individuals only come together to mate. Rhinos have poor eyesight and will often charge, seemingly without reason. Creatures of habit, they have a well-defined home range and make daily trips to a watering hole where they are occasionally attacked by lions, more often by poachers.

* * *

In 1749, when Jean-Baptiste Oudry painted Clara, the most famous rhinoceros who ever lived, she was halfway through her seventeen year tour of Europe. She visited dozens of cities and created a sensation wherever she went as she was only the fifth rhinoceros to be seen in Europe since the rhinoceros that became the subject of Albrecht Dürer's woodcut in 1515. Oudry's Clara was larger than life, in a canvas that measured ten feet by fifteen feet. Solitary, in the foreground of a bucolic landscape of mountains and lakes, Clara seems to eye the viewer with an air of regality mixed with world-weariness.

* * *

Everyone wants your attention, wander alone like a rhinoceros.

* * *

Of the five extant species, all endangered, extinction seems inevitable for the Sumatran and Javan rhino, numbering only a few hundred or a few dozen members. The white rhino was nearly hunted to extinction a century ago, its numbers dwindling to less than a hundred, but in a conservation success, its numbers have now risen to more than 14,000. However, poachers, interested in the rhino horn for the traditional Chinese medicine trade, have nearly wiped out the northern white rhino population in the Congo. The Indian rhino has also rebounded from perilously low numbers early in the 20th century to about 2600 today. The situation remains critical for the black rhino, which numbered as high as 70,000 in the late 1960s and now sits around 3500. The western black rhino, formerly of Cameroon, was poached to extinction in 2011.

* * *

Cold and heat, hunger and thirst, wander alone like a rhinoceros.

* * *

In a letter to his grandmother in 1838, Charles Darwin, then a young man, reports on seeing a rhinoceros at the zoo:

> by the greatest piece of good fortune it was the first time this year the Rhinoceros was turned out. – Such a sight has seldom been seen as to behold the rhinoceros kicking and rearing (though neither end reached any great height) out of joy. – it galloped up & down its court surprisingly quickly, like a huge cow, & it was marvelous how suddenly it could stop & turn around at the end of each gallop. – The elephant was in the adjoining yard & was greatly amused at seeing the rhinoceros so frisky.

* * *

In Japanese writer Kaoru Maruyana's poem "A Rhinoceros and a Lion," a lion clings to the back of a running rhinoceros, biting; blood spurts. The rhino twists its neck upward, in agony. High above the mute landscape, the daytime moon floats. Caught in a frieze of time:

> The lion was, moment by moment, trying to kill;
> The rhinoceros was, eternally, about to die.

The Zanzibar Leopard
Panthera pardus adersi

The leopard has an unhappy history on Zanzibar. For awhile it was revered as a king, kept by elders to demonstrate their authority. Wild leopards were little seen, haunting the thickets in the coral-country on the east side of the island. When the population spread, the leopards' rarity fuelled superstitions: they were thought to be under control of wizards who punished victims by sending them at will to carry off their fowls or goats. They were feared as man-eaters and shape-shifters, and because of the increasing conflict between humans and leopards as the leopards lost habitat, they were demonized. A person could be cursed and become a leopard—a fate worse than any disease in the world. Locals built large wooden traps and when an unfortunate leopard was captured, its eyes were seared to break the spell before it was dispatched.

A poem from the Yoruba touches on both the reverences and superstitions of this magnificent beast that lurked on the fringes of the imagination of the island.

Gentle hunter
his tail plays on the ground
while he crushes the skull.
Beautiful death
who puts on a spotted robe
when he goes to his victim
Playful killer
whose loving embrace
splits the antelope's heart.

VIII.
Lost Animals of the Indian Ocean

"The Dodo seems to afford us an example of the extinction of an animal in comparatively recent times."

– Henry Thomas de la Beche, *A Geological Manual*, 1831

* * *

Together, the Mascarene Islands have lost more than fifty species.

The Dodo
Raphus cucullatus

Though the dodo had been painted while still alive, and some birds were brought to Europe as curiosities, after its extinction in the 1660s, it lapsed into obscurity and was only infrequently mentioned as an example of a species that had become extinct, an idea that was still unpopular in scientific circles. In the mid-19th century, the dodo came back to life, as it were, beginning with a popular article in *The Penny Magazine* in 1833, which drove home the reality of extinction and the human agency. A monograph, *The Dodo and Its Kindred*, soon followed, which was well-reviewed and a life-sized dodo reconstruction went on display at the Great Exhibition in London in 1851. In 1860, the Oxford museum prominently displayed its dodo remains along with a painting of the bird by Jan Savery. Charles Dodgson, better known as Lewis Carroll, was a frequent visitor to the museum and was sufficiently inspired to include two illustrations of the dodo in *Alice in Wonderland* in 1865. His self-referential characterization of the dodo as well as the illustrations helped propel the dodo into the mainstream as an icon of extinction.

An anonymous contemporary account from 1631 indicates some of the character of the bird and who ran the island in the absence of humans:

> These mayors are superb and proud. They displayed themselves to us with stiff and stern faces, and wide-open mouths. Jaunty and audacious of gait, they would scarcely move a foot before us. Their war weapon was their mouth, with which they could bite fiercely; their food was fruit; they were not well feathered but abundantly covered with fat. Many of them were brought onboard to the delight of us all.

Unfortunately, this delight was not for the character of the bird, but for something new to eat.

Later maligned as stupid, the pudgy, large-headed and large-beaked dodo was instead curious and, like many island birds, unafraid of humans. "These animals on our coming up to them stared at us and remained quiet where they stand," wrote Volkert Evertsz, a Dutch sailor shipwrecked on Mauritius in 1662, "and suffering us to approach them as close as we pleased." This tameness was used against the birds: "I held one by the leg. He let out a cry and others came forward to help the prisoner." Other dodos were then also caught. As the island had no permanent settlement at that time, these sailors were some of the last people to see the dodo alive.

The Giant Tortoises of the Mascarenes
Cylindraspis indica, C. inepta, C. vosmaeri, C. peltastes, C. triserrata

Long ago, perhaps many thousands of years, a few giant tortoises on Madagascar entered the Indian Ocean to see where the currents would take them. They floated for weeks like a small flotilla of helmets bobbing up and down in the waves, until the currents washed them ashore on the Mascarene Islands, five hundred miles to the east. When they arrived, their legs and giant shells—domed or saddle-backed—were covered with barnacles, as if they were driftwood.

With average ages surpassing a century and tortoises often living more than two hundred years, these were the wise old masters of the Earth. Probably washed offshore during a storm, it's still tempting to think that they entered the ocean deliberately, seeking more fertile ground, as it were, devoid of predators. They took to their new home readily—the volcanic islands of Mauritius, Réunion and Rodrigues had only appeared a few million years before—and grew to enormous size. In 1631, an Englishman described their size as "so great that they will creepe with two mens burthen;" sketches from around that time show two men reclining comfortably on the back of a tortoise.

During the heat of the day they would pile up on top of each other in the shade, desperate to get out of the sun for overheating would be deadly. Sometimes they travelled together in giant herds of a few thousand, as if they all got the same idea at once to visit a local watering hole or to rest somewhere in the evening, and were each executing it in their own mindful way.

The end took little over a century and a half. The earliest settlers in the 17th century, particularly on Mauritius, exploited them for food as a tastier alternative to the dodo. When seafarers discovered the tortoises could be stored live on ships with little food or water for months on end, they purchased hundreds at a time for long voyages. Storing the animals upside down induced a state of surrender. Loss of the tortoise from Réunion in 1754 did not halt the practice and the giant tortoise was lost from Mauritius in 1778 and Rodrigues in 1795.

It's difficult to picture their former abundance but naturalist Francois Leguat gives a clue in 1691 on Rodrigues: "there are such plenty of Land-Turtles in this isle that sometimes you see two or three thousand of them in a flock, so that you may go above a hundred paces on their backs... without setting foot on the ground." Elsewhere he writes that the area seemed "paved with them."

Leguat also remarks on a puzzling but endearing quality: after the herd has migrated, "they always place sentinels at some distance from their troop, at the four corners of their camp, to which the sentinels turn their backs and look with the eyes, as if they were on a watch." It's almost cartoonish to think that a tortoise on a watch could do much good, as most predators could easily evade it. The puzzle of what they were watching for in their plodding, slow-motion world remains.

The Mascarene Blue Pigeons
Alectroenas nitidissima (Mauritius)
A. payandeei (Rodrigues)
A. sp. (Réunion)

Perhaps they came from the East, island-hopping into the Indian Ocean, not all at once but in waves, descended from ancestral Asian fruit doves. When some islands later succumbed to tectonic activity and submerged, the birds flew again west to the Mascarenes, the Seychelles, and Madagascar. Until one day, after so many successive variations, deep in the evergreen mountain forests or along the river valleys, solitary or in groups, one finds this being of avian loveliness: deep metallic blue plumage, a maroon tail, a red patch on its forehead, and a magnificent collar of white feathers adorning its head, neck and breast that could be raised at will. And so it did, raised its hackles into a ruff, an alluring display for a mate. With that, the cooing came gently and often.

Rodrigues Solitaire
Pezophaps solitaria

The females are wonderfully beautiful, some fair, some brown; I call them fair because they are the colour of fair Hair. They have a sort of Peak like a Widow's upon their Breasts, which is of a dusky Colour.

* * *

Taller and more slender than the closely related dodo, the solitaire was championed by Huguenot exile François Leguat who lived on Rodrigues from 1691 to 1693 and whose accounts of the bird were so elegiac later scientists doubted their veracity.

* * *

No one feather is straggling from the other over all their Bodies, they being careful to adjust themselves and make them all even with their Beaks.

* * *

The solitaire lived alongside a unique menagerie of island species that followed it into extinction: the Rodrigues rail, the Rodrigues parrot, Newton's parakeet, the Rodrigues starling, the Rodrigues owl, the Rodrigues night heron, the Rodrigues pigeon.

* * *

They have two Risings on their Craws, and the Feathers are whiter than the rest, which livelily Represents the fine Neck of a Beautiful Woman.

* * *

They strutted proudly about, alone or in pairs. After mating, the female laid a single egg, larger than a goose's, and she and the male took turns covering it. Fiercely territorial, if a male intruder came, the female would flutter her wings and call her mate to send it away. If a female intruded, the male would flutter *his* wings, and call the female to repel it.

* * *

They walk with so much Stateliness and good Grace, that one cannot help admiring and loving them, to the extent that quite often their good Appearance has saved their Lives.

After the offspring has fledged, a group of solitaires brings another fledgling to it and they all march to some distant place. *Afterwards the old ones went each their way alone, or in Couples, and left the two young ones together, which we call'd a Marriage.*

* * *

For almost fifty years over the turn of the 19th century, the solitaire was commemorated with a constellation of stars in the region of Libra, Hydra and Scorpio, though on star atlases, a thrush was pictured instead of the solitaire. The idea fell into disuse in the 1820s and the stars were regrouped into their original constellations. Despite the misidentification, it's still the only extinct species to have flown, however briefly, in the heavens.

* * *

Leguat remarked on the ease of catching the solitaire, and the sad outcome: *They will never grow Tame: as soon as they are caught they shed Tears without Crying and refuse all manner of Sustenance till they die.*

The Round Island Burrowing Boa
Bolyeria multocarinata
Sneaking through the shaded soil of the palm groves down the volcanic slopes, sampling the air with forked tongue efficiency, seeking hospitality in the hot, hot sun from out the dark door of the secret Earth, seen only four times in a century, his shovel-shaped head and cylindrical body burrowing into the soil and out of sight.

CODA

"We need another and a wiser and perhaps a more mystical concept of animals. Remote from universal nature, and living by complicated artifice, man in civilization surveys the creature through the glass of his knowledge and sees thereby a feather magnified and the whole image in distortion. We patronize them for their incompleteness, for their tragic fate of having taken form so far below ourselves. And therein we err, and greatly err. For the animal shall not be measured by man. In a world older and more complex than ours they move finished and complete, gifted with extensions of the senses we have lost or never attained, living by voices we shall never hear. They are not brethren, they are not underlings; they are other nations, caught with ourselves in the net of life and time, fellow prisoners of the splendour and travail of the earth."

– Henry Beston, *The Outermost House*, 1928

* * *

When they gave the roll-call for the animals who were endangered, those who could still be saved, so many didn't answer when their name was called that a silence set in over the landscape.

APPENDIX A

List of Species Grouped by Taxonomic Classification

AMPHIBIANS

18   Ainsworth's Salamander (North America)

54   Andean Black Toad (South America)

57   Chile Darwin Frog (South America)

23   Coquis of Puerto Rico (North America/Caribbean)

80   Gastric-brooding Frog (Australia and New Zealand)

58   Golden Toad (Central America)

59   Rabb's Fringe-limbed Tree Frog (Central America)

60   Scrawny Stubfoot Toad (South America)

93   Shrub Frogs of Sri Lanka (Asia)

96   Yunnan Lake Newt (Asia)

ANNELIDS

102   Lake Pedder Earthworm (Australia/Tasmania)

BIRDS

54   Atitlán Grebe (Central America/Guatemala)

19   Bachman's Warbler (North America)

40   Black Mamo (Hawaii and the Pacific Islands)

22   Carolina Parakeet (North America)

74   Chatham Island Bellbird (Australia and New Zealand)

76   Chatham Island Rails (Australia and New Zealand)

54   Colombian Grebe (South America)

110   Dodo (Indian Ocean/Mauritius)

23   Dusky Seaside Sparrow (North America)

24   Eskimo Curlew (North/South America)

57   Glaucous Macaw (South America)

CNIDARIANS

ECHINODERMS

FISH

INSECTS

JAWLESS FISH (CEPHALASPIDOMORPHS)

MAMMALS

APPENDIX B

References and Notes on the Extinction of Individual Species

Among the historical, scientific and literary texts I consulted when doing background reading for the entries in this book, I made particularly extensive use of David Day's *Doomsday Book of Animals* (Ebury Press, 1981), Tim Flannery's *A Gap in Nature: Discovering the World's Extinct Animals* (Atlantic Monthly Press, 2001) and Julian Hume's *Extinct Birds* (Poyser Monographs, 2012). I also regularly consulted the IUCN Red List (iucnredlist.org) and Peter Maas's *The Sixth Extinction* website, www.petermaas.nl/extinct.

1. Ainsworth's Salamander. The oldest oceanic crust in the Atlantic is about 180 million years old. *Tyrannosaurus rex* lived from about 68 to 65 million years ago. The oldest flowering plants are about 140 million years old, slightly younger than the split of lungless salamanders from their next closest relatives about 145 million years ago.

    James Lazell's discovery paper is "A New Salamander in the Genus *Plethodon* from Mississippi," in *Copeia*, vol. 1998, #4, pp. 967-70.

2. Amistad Gambusia. Extinction due to habitat modification when the silt-laden water that created the Amistad Reservoir inundated its spring in 1968.

3. Andean Black Toad. A member of the large genus of true toads, commonly known as harlequin or stubfoot toads, found in the neotropics from Costa Rica to Bolivia. Most of the species in the genus have suffered dramatic declines due to the chytrid fungus, compounded by drought in protected areas caused by climate change. This species has not been recorded since 1988.

    Description based on James A. Peters' "The Frog Genus *Atelopus* in Ecuador (Anura: Bufonidae)," *Smithsonian Contributions to Zoology*, 1973, Number 145, 24-7.

4. Aurochs. Aurochs is singular, the plural is aurochsen.

5. Australian Hopping Mice. Before European settlers arrived, there were ten species of hopping mice and now only five remain. Primary causes of extinction are habitat alteration for agriculture and predation by introduced foxes and cats.

    The short-tailed hopping mouse lived near Alice Springs and was last seen in 1896.

    The long-tailed hopping mouse lived broadly in western and central Australia and was last collected in 1901.

The big-eared hopping mouse lived in the Moore River area of south-western Australia and was last collected in Perth in 1843.

The Darling Downs hopping mouse is known from a single skull collected in the named farming region of southern Queensland in the 1840s.

The great hopping mouse is only known from skulls found in owl pellets in the Flinders Ranges of southern Australia; it probably went extinct in the second half of the 19th century.

6. Bachman's Warbler. First collected by John Bachman in 1832 and became rare after clear-cutting was introduced to its habitat around the turn of the 20th century. Became rare in the 1930s though sightings continued until the 1970s. Not officially extinct as some habitat remains that has not been surveyed, in Congaree National Park, South Carolina. The piece here is based on eyewitness reports published in *The Auk* in the early part of the 20th century.

7. Baiji. Last sighted in 2004, the baiji was a victim of pollution, electric fishing, increased boat traffic and general habitat destruction due to the increasing population around the Yangzte River.

8. Banff Longnose Dace. Mosquitofish were introduced into the dace's habitat in the 1920s; it disappeared in 1986.

9. Birds of Guadalupe. Goats were first brought to the island in the 19th century and the birds disappeared within a few decades. The goat population peaked at around 100,000; the last ones were eradicated in 2005 by the Mexican government so that the island is now a biosphere preserve.

The storm petrel disappeared in the 1910s. Bewick's wren and the spotted towhee went extinct in the late 1890s; the caracara around 1901.

See "The Present State of the Ornis of Guadaloupe Island" by John E. Thayer and Outram Bangs, *The Condor*, vol 10, no. 3 (May – June 1908), pp. 101-6. The Bryant quote is taken from "Additions to the Ornithology of Guadalupe Island" in *Bulletin of the California Academy of Sciences*, vol 11 (5-8), 1887, p. 282.

10. Black Mamo. Quote from Julian Hume's *Extinct Birds* (2012). Despite the described hunting story, the black mamo, a species of honeycreeper, was driven to extinction by habitat destruction, introduced rats and mosquito-borne diseases.

11. Bluebuck. The first large African mammal to become extinct in modern times, the bluebuck had a limited range in the coastal plains on the southern tip of South Africa. After European settlement, it lost much of its habitat to agriculture, and was ultimately

hunted to extinction around 1800. See Graham Renshaw's *Final Natural History Essays,* Sherratt and Hughes, 1907.

12. Bubal Hartebeest. Hunted to extinction in 1954. Description from Graham Renshaw's *Final Natural History Essays,* Sherratt and Hughes, 1907, and *The Cama or Hartebeest,* digitized by the University of Pretoria Library Services, 2013, original date unknown.

13. Cape Verde Giant Skink. Not seen since early in the 20th century, the giant skink suffered from hunting, droughts, being used by stranded convicts for food and over-collection by museum collectors.

14. Caribbean Monk Seal. Last seen in 1952, after being over-hunted for its oil.

15. Carolina Parakeet. Extinction due to overhunting. The last Carolina parakeet died in 1918. Passages after German immigrant Gert Goebel, 1877, and C.J. Maynard, 1896, quoted in Christopher Cokinos' *Hope Is the Thing with Feathers.*

16. Chatham Island Bellbird. On Captain Cook's voyage to Tahiti to observe the transit of Venus, his naturalist Joseph Banks made these observations about the Chatham Island Bellbird in 1770: "I was awakened by the singing of birds ashore from whence we are distant not a quarter of a mile. Their numbers were certainly very great. They seemed to strain their throats with emulation and made perhaps the most melodious wild music I have ever heard, almost imitating silver bells, but with the most tunable silver sound imaginable to which may be the distance was no small addition." (Day 1981)

Cook himself described them similarly: "it seemed to be like small bells exquisitely tuned." Last sighted in 1906, the Chatham Island bellbird was driven to extinction by introduced cats, rats and forest destruction, as well as museum collectors.

The Chatham Islands are about 680 kilometers southeast of New Zealand.

17. Chatham Island Rails. Extinction due to introduced rats and cats, as well as the indigenous practice of slash-and-burn agriculture, which destroyed their habitat. Dieffenbach was the only naturalist to see "his" rail, in 1940. The Chatham rail, discovered in 1872, was last collected just twenty-one years later, in 1893. See the website New Zealand Birds Online, at nzbirdsonline.org.nz.

18. Chile Darwin Frog. Last seen in 1980, the Chile Darwin frog was one of two species of mouth-brooding frogs originally discovered by Charles Darwin in 1834 on his voyage on the *Beagle.* Darwin is said to have called it "pretty and curious" though he didn't note it in his official journal. The Chile Darwin frog, also known as the northern Darwin frog, suffered from the chytrid fungus and possibly habitat destruction.

Another species, the southern Darwin frog, *Rhinoderma darwinii,* survives in southern Chile and Argentina, but is also endangered from the chytrid fungus.

19. Chinese Paddlefish. Over the 20ᵗʰ century, the population of the Chinese paddlefish, whose evolutionary lineage dates back 400 million years and could grow to over twenty feet long, decreased due to overfishing and habitat degradation. In 1981, the erection of the Gezhouba Dam in the middle of the Yangzte blocked its migration route. Only two adults have been recorded since 2002 and juveniles were last seen in 1995. *Marvel at the changed world* is from the poem "Swimming" by Mao Zedong; the last lines are from Tu Fu's poem "Traveling at Night."

20. Christmas Island Mammals. Description based on *Extinct and Vanishing Animals of the Old World* by Francis Harper, 1945, New York, American Committee for International Wildlife Protection, and "Account of Christmas Island, Indian Ocean" by W. J. L. Wharton, *Proceedings of the Royal Geographical Society and Monthly Record of Geography,* New Monthly Series, vol 10, no. 10 (Oct. 1888), pp. 613-24.

   Strong evidence that the two rat species were wiped out by disease is presented in Wyatt KB, Campos PF, Gilbert MTP, Kolokotronis S-O, Hynes WH, et al. (2008) "Historical Mammal Extinction on Christmas Island (Indian Ocean) Correlates with Introduced Infectious Disease." *PLoS ONE* 3(11): e3602.

   Reasons for the decline of the shrew are uncertain, though the introduced diseased rats could have been potent, as well as the introduction of feral cats and loss of habitat due to agriculture. See "The Decline and Current Status of the Christmas Island Shrew *Crocidura Attenuata Trichura* on Christmas Island, Indian Ocean" by Paul D. Meek, *Australian Mammology,* 22:43-9.

   The pipistrelle population began to decline in the mid-1980s, though there had been little change in habitat to warrant the change in numbers. A possible reason for extinction is disturbances by introduced species while nesting, including the common wolf snake, feral cats, the black rat and giant centipedes. Named after Scottish naturalist John Murray, who, together with G. Clunies Ross, opened the phosphate mine that operated for much of the 20ᵗʰ century.

21. Coquis of Puerto Rico. The genus *Eleutherodactylus* ("free-toed") had 17 species on Puerto Rico and the three missing species had their own songs, different from the *ko-kee* sound that is heard all over the island. Habitat destruction and the chytrid fungus are thought to be reasons for the frogs' disappearance.

   Jasper Loftus-Hills was a promising 28-year-old Australian naturalist who was taping frog calls along a Texas highway in 1974 when he was killed by a hit-and-run driver. He helped discover the golden coqui in 1973 and his colleagues named the frog in his honor, *Eleutherodactylus jasperi.*

22. Desert Rat-Kangaroo. Discovered in the 1840s and not seen again until the 1931 and thought to be extinct in the interim. Last seen in 1935. Well-adapted to its harsh environment and driven to extinction by habitat alteration and the introduction of feral cats and European red foxes.

    Account based on Hedley Finlayson (quoted in Hume's *Extinct Birds*), who found a thriving colony in 1931 and sought to study them. After the described chase, the oolacunta died from exhaustion; other chases ended similarly, which prompted Finlayson to say that it was "incredible that so small a frame should be capable of such immense output of energy... All examples behaved similarly... They persisted to the very limit of their strength, and quite literally, they paused only to die."

23. Dodo. It is said that Charles Dodgson took a liking to the bird because of his stammer ("Do-do-dodgson"). Hunting was one cause of its extinction, together with the introduction of dogs, rats, cats, pigs and macaques to the island, which raided its nests.

    See "The Dodo's last island—where did Volkert Evertsz meet the last wild dodos?" by Anthony Cheke, in *Proceedings of the Royal Society of the Arts and Sciences of Mauritius*, vol 7, 2004, pp. 7-22.

24. Dusky Seaside Sparrow. "Orange Band" died on June 17, 1987, a victim of pollution and habitat destruction. The story is inspired by a photo by photographer Joel Sartore, founder of The Photo Ark (joelsartore.com/galleries/the-photo-ark).

25. Eskimo Curlew. Once one of the most numerous shore birds in North America; hunted to extinction. See "Where Have All the Curlews Gone?" by Paul A. Johnsgard, *Papers in Ornithology*, Paper 23, 1980.

26. Ethiopian Water Mouse. Extinction due to habitat loss (conversion to pastureland) sometime after the collection of the only specimen in the 1920s.

27. Falkland Islands Wolf. Extinction due to overhunting.

28. Freshwater Mussels of North America. North America is home to the greatest freshwater mussel diversity in the world, with about 300 species; for comparison, there are about 85 species in Africa and 11 species in Europe. Mussels began to be over-harvested in the 19th century for pearls and then in the early 20th century for the shell-button industry. Almost all of the extinctions recorded here are from the mid-to-late 20th century due to direct loss of habitat by stream impoundment or channelization or indirect effects of fragmentation due to habitat destruction. Mussels parasitize certain host fish when they are young and depend on free-flowing streams and rivers so they can filter out food that passes by. Changes in rivers that affect the fish population or the clarity and speed of the rivers, including pollution, agricultural runoff, dredging,

increased sedimentation, and damming have large and negative impacts on mussel populations and it is likely that 25% or more of the North American mussel fauna will be extinct within a human generation. As a group, mollusks (including mussels, clams, snails and slugs) comprise about one-third of the extinctions since the year 1500.

See Wendell R. Haag, "Past and future patterns of freshwater mussel extinctions in North America during the Holocene," in *Holocene Extinctions*, edited by Samuel R. Turvey, Oxford University Press, 2009.

29. Gastric-brooding Frog. Extinction probably due to the chytrid fungus.

30. Giant Tortoises of the Mascarene Islands. In the Indian Ocean, giant tortoises were spared destruction on Aldabra Island, north of Madagascar in the Seychelles, because of its remoteness. Tortoises from Aldabra are now being used to re-populate the Mascarene Islands.

Leguat is quoted in *A Sheltered Life: The Unexpected History of the Giant Tortoise*, by Paul Chambers, p. 17.

The Englishman is quoted in *The Song of the Dodo: Island Biogeography in an Age of Extinction* by David Quammen, p. 123.

31. Glaucous Macaw. Became rare in the 19th century due to hunting, its popularity as a pet and loss of habitat; formerly found mostly in northern Argentina and adjacent areas but only two sightings were recorded in the 20th century. See *Spix's Macaw: The Race to Save the World's Rarest Bird* by Tony Juniper, Fourth Estate, 2003.

32. Golden Toad. Last seen in 1989. Extinction possibly due to climate change, El Niño (which caused the pools to dry up early) and the chytrid fungus.

33. Great Auk. Extinction due to overhunting. Description and quotes from "The Breeding Ecology and Extinction of the Great Auk (*Pinguinus impennis*): Anecdotal Evidence and Conjectures" in *The Auk*, vol 101, no. 1, Jan. 1984, by Sven-Axel Bengtson, and *Great Auk Islands; a field biologist in the Arctic*, by Tim Birkhead, Poyser Monographs, 2010.

34. Greater Akialoa. Last seen in the 1960s on Kaua'i. According to the IUCN, other islands lost their subspecies of akialoas earlier, due to forest destruction and mosquito-borne avian diseases. With the disappearance of the lesser akialoa (*Hemignathus obscurans*) from the island of Hawaii in 1940, the entire genus is now gone.

This piece was inspired by a quote from George Munro, quoted in Hume (2012).

35. Greater Short-tailed Bat. Bats are the only mammals endemic to New Zealand and the short-tailed bats are thought to have arrived some 26 million years ago from Australia, while long-tailed bats were more recent arrivals. After Polynesians settlers introduced rats to the main islands, the greater short-tailed bat survived only on Big South

Cape Island and adjoining islands to the south of New Zealand. However, rats were introduced there too in 1962 and wiped out many species that had taken refuge there, creating a modern ecological disaster. The greater short-tailed bat was last seen in 1967. The closely related lesser short-tailed bat survives today, primarily on the South Island of New Zealand.

36. Grebes. The last two Atitlán grebes were seen in 1989, and the Colombian grebe was last seen in the 1970s.

37. Guam Flying Fox. A local delicacy in the Marianas, the Guam flying fox was hunted to extinction in the 1960s.

38. Gull Island Vole. Extinction in 1898 due to habitat destruction.

39. Harelip Sucker. Formerly found in the clear streams of the upper Mississippi Valley, and the Lake Erie and Ohio drainage basins.

    See Williams, J.D. and Nowak, R. M., *Vanishing Species in our Own Backyard: Extinct Fish and Wildlife of the United States and Canada* in *The Last Extinction*, edited by Les Kaufman and Kenneth Mallory, MIT Press, 1986. For its feeding habits, see Fink, W.L. and Humphries, J. H., "Morphological Description of the Extinct North American Sucker *Moxostoma lacerum* (Ostariophysi, Catostomidae), Based on High-Resolution X-Ray Computed Tomography" in *Copeia*, vol. 2010, 1, 5-13.

40. Hawaiian Rail. Extinction due to introduced dogs, cats and rats.

41. Heath Hen. Formerly common throughout Colonial times, from Maine to North Carolina, and many have speculated that they, not wild turkeys, comprised the Pilgrims' first Thanksgiving meal. Hunted extensively for food until they were extirpated from the mainland by the middle of the 19th century, the last ones thrived on Martha's Vineyard, an island off Cape Cod, Massachusetts. Despite protective measures, the numbers continued to decline and a series of factors during the final decades, such as a forest fire during one of the mating seasons, poultry disease, predation by goshawks and feral cats and inbreeding led to the species' extinction in 1932.

    Description based on Edward Howe Forbush's 1918 article in *The American Museum Journal.*

42. Huia. One of New Zealand's iconic birds, the huia was last collected in 1907, with sightings at least until the 1920s. Extinction due to over hunting, for its tail feathers, and to habitat loss as old growth forest was converted to land for agriculture by European settlers. Introduced rats, cats and mustelids (weasels, ferrets and stoats) may have also contributed as the huia spent much time on the ground and nested in old dead trees.

    Description based on Clark Monson's article, "Cultural Constraints and Corrosive

Colonization: Western Commerce in Aotearoa/New Zealand and the Extinction of the Huia (*Heteralocha acutirostris*)," *Pacific Studies*, 2005, 28 (1/2): 68–93, which uses first-hand reports from Walter Buller and Thomas Potts.

43. Ilin Island Cloudrunner. Extinction due to forest destruction. Last seen in 1953. Ilin Island is directly south of the island of Mindoro in the Philippines.

44. Ivell's Sea Anemone. Sea anemones belong to the phylum Cnidaria (nid-AIR-ee-a), whose fossil record dates back more than 550 million years. They were the first animals to have muscles and nerves to produce behavior. Ivell's sea anemone is only known from the Widewater Lagoon, West Sussex, England. Discovered in 1975, the water quality in the lagoon degraded from pesticide and fertilizer run-off from nearby gardens, and it has not been seen since 1983 despite several searches. It is classed by the IUCN as Data Deficient.

45. Ivory-billed Woodpecker. Most were wiped out in the late 19th century by logging and hunting by collectors. Few were seen after the 1920s. The IUCN classifies it as Critically Endangered Possibly Extinct, and, tantalizing as reports of sightings may be, any surviving individuals must be very few.

46. Japanese Sea Lion. Annual harvests of about 3,200 at the turn of the 20th century fell to about 300 by 1915 and a few dozen by the early 1930s, after which they were thought to be extinct. They were also shot by Japanese fishermen for interfering with their catch. One cave they were observed in was on Ulleungdo Island but for the most part, their behavior went unstudied; they are thought to be similar to the California sea lion, upon which much of this description is based.

   See Richard S. Peterson and George A. Bartholomew, "Natural History and Behavior of the California Sea Lion," American Society of Mammalogists, *Special Pub.* #1, Dec 5, 1967. See also the historical documents and accounts regarding the sea lions of Liancourt Island at dokdo-or-takeshima.blogspot.com.

47. Japanese River Otter. Once numbering in the millions, the Japanese river otter was overhunted for its fur and also suffered as its river habitat became polluted and urbanized. The last official sighting was in 1979. See "Japanese River Otter Declared Extinct" by John R. Platt, published at scientificamerican.com on Sept. 5, 2012. The last line quotes Seamus Heaney's poem, "The Otter".

48. Javan Tiger. Inspired by a similar essay in Weinberger's *An Elemental Thing*.

49. Labrador Duck. Extinct in the 1870s, though the reason is uncertain, possibly due to over-harvesting of eggs or a decline in the shellfish population, on which the birds fed.

50. Lake Hadley Sticklebacks. According to biologist Todd Hatfield, "The loss of

opportunity for further study of the Hadley Lake species pair is widely recognized as a scientific tragedy." (2001) A similar pair in Enos Lake, Vancouver Island recently hybridized due to the introduction of crayfish. Other species pairs exist in lakes on Texada Island and are listed as Threatened by the Committee on the Status of Endangered Wildlife in Canada.

Above quote and information from Todd Hatfield, 2001, "Status of the stickleback species pair, *Gasterosteus* spp. in Hadley Lake, Lasqueti Island, British Columbia," *Canadian Field Naturalist*, 115: 579-83.

51. Lake Alaotra Grebe. The last was seen in 1985.

52. Lake Pedder Earthworm. Known from a single specimen collected in 1971 on a main beach of Lake Pedder, Tasmania, the pale-brown worm was a few inches long and had 129 body segments. It became extinct in 1972 when the lake was dammed for hydroelectricity.

53. Lake Victoria Cichlids. See "Cichlids of the Rift Lakes" by Melanie L.J. Stiassny and Axel Meyer, *Scientific American*, Feb. 1999, pp. 64-9, and "The Holocene History of Lake Victoria" by T.C. Johnson, K. Kelts and E. Okada, *Ambio*, vol 29, #1 (Feb. 2000), pp. 2-11. See also the film *Darwin's Nightmare*.

54. Laughing Owl. The last known laughing owl died in 1914, a victim of museum collectors, habitat loss and introduced predators such as stoats, ferrets and cats, from which it had no defense.

55. Laysan Honeycreeper. Last seen in 1923; extinction due to loss of habitat from the introduction of rabbits. The Tanager Expedition is described in detail in *Atoll Research Bulletin* No. 433, "History and Ornithological Journals of the *Tanager* Expedition of 1923 to the Northwestern Hawaiian Islands, Johnson and Wake Islands" by Storrs L. Olson, 1996. Additional information from "The Present Status of the Birds of Hawaii" by Andrew J. Berger, in *Pacific Science*, vol 24. pp. 29-42, Jan. 1970.

56. Laysan Millerbird. Extinction due to introduced rabbits, which denuded the island, wiping out the millerbird's vegetative protection and its main food source, three species of moths. Quote from Day (1981).

57. Laysan Millers. Extinction due to introduced rabbits, as described above. Description based on German naturalist Hugo H. Schauinsland's article, "Three Months on a Coral Island (Laysan)" [1899], *Atoll Research Bulletin*, No. 432, translated by Miklos D.F. Udvardy.

58. Laysan Rail. Extinction due to introduced rabbits, which denuded the island, wiping out the bird's vegetative protection and the moths and insects, such as the brine fly, it

depended on. Last seen in 1923.

59. Lesser Bilby. Last seen in the 1950s, or possibly the 1960s, the lesser bilby suffered from introduced foreign predators like the domestic cat and fox. Description based on *Extinct and Vanishing Animals of the Old World* by Francis Harper, 1945, New York, American Committee for International Wildlife Protection, and *No Turning Back* by Richard Ellis, HarperCollins, 2005.

60. Little Swan Island Hutia. The Swan Islands are the most isolated islands in the Caribbean and Little Swan Island is only 1.5 miles long and 0.3 miles wide. Numerous until the mid-20th century, the hutia declined with the introduction of goats to the island, as well as cats and none were seen after the 1955 hurricane.

    Out of twenty species of hutia in the Caribbean, a third have gone extinct since European settlement.

    Description and quote from "Geocapromys thoracatus" by Gary S. Morgan, *Mammalian Species,* no. 341, pp. 1-5.

61. Madeiran Large White. According to Peter Maas at the Sixth Extinction website, the Madeiran large white's numbers declined due to loss of habitat from human encroachment. Pollution from agricultural fertilizers may have also played a role. The IUCN website says the cause of extinction is unknown, but speculates about introduction of diseases or parasites as possible causes.

62. Mamo. Though it is said that 80,000 birds were sacrificed for King Kamehameha I's resplendent yellow cloak, it is more likely that habitat destruction and disease were the cause of its extinction.

63. Maryland Darter. Extinction in the 1980s from alteration of habitat.

64. Mascarene Blue Pigeons. The blue pigeon became extinct on Mauritius in the 1830s due to the deforestation that occurred during French rule (1715-1810). The blue pigeon was not described by contemporary writers on Réunion or Rodrigues and is only known from fossils, hence its extinction date is uncertain. Blue pigeons survive on the Seychelles, Madagascar and the Comoros Islands.

    Some scenarios for pigeon diversification are presented in "Mitochondrial and Nuclear DNA Sequences Support a Cretaceous Origin of Columbiformes and a Dispersal-Driven Radiation in the Paleogene" by Sergio L. Pereira, Kevin P. Johnson, Dale H. Clayton and Allan J. Baker, *Systematic Biology,* 2007, 56 (4), 656-72. Additional information from *Lost Land of the Dodo: The Ecological History of Mauritius, Réunion and Rodrigues* by Anthony Cheke and Julian P. Hume, A and C Black, London, pp. 167-8.

65. Monarchs of French Polynesia. The islands of French Polynesia, including Tahiti (part of the Society Islands) and the Marquesas, are thought to have a range of ages up to six million years old and Cibois *et al.* argue that monarchs colonized the islands within a million years of their formation.

Monarch species survive on several of the other islands though the Tahiti monarch (*Pomarea nigra*) and Fatuhiva monarch (*P. whitneyi*) are critically endangered. Many of these birds are known from the Whitney South Seas Expedition of the 1920s. The Maupiti monarch (*P. pomarea*) is known from only one specimen collected in 1822 as well as a painting, and it disappeared soon after. The others were last seen in the 1970s, while the Ua Pou monarch (*P. mira*) disappeared in 1985. Little is known of their biology or habits, though they are thought to be similar to the Tahiti monarch.

The evolutionary history of Polynesian monarchs is presented in "Biogeography of Eastern Polynesian Monarchs (*Pomarea*): An Endemic Genus Close to Extinction" by Alice Cibois, Jean-Claude Thibault and Eric Pasquet, *The Condor*, Vol. 106, No. 4 (Nov., 2004), pp. 837-51.

66. Miss Waldron's Red Colobus Monkey. Last official sighting in 1978; extinction due to poaching for bushmeat and habitat destruction. Yoruba hunter poems can be found in *The Rattle Bag*, edited by Seamus Heaney and Ted Hughes, Faber and Faber, 1982.

67. Oahu Tree Snails. These extinctions occurred throughout the 20th century. The rosy wolf snail (*Euglandina rosea*) was introduced in 1955 to control another snail, which had become an agricultural pest.

See "How Many Hawaiian Land Snail Species Are Left and What Can We Do for Them?" by Alan Solem, in *Bishop Museum Occasional Papers*, vol. 30, June 1990, pp. 27-40.

68. Ō'ō. The Kaua'i o'o (*Moho braccatus*) was said to be one of Hawaii's finest singers. It was last seen in 1987. Other islands had their own species of ō'ō and they disappeared much earlier, probably from avian malaria, introduced predators and habitat loss. They were: the Oahu ō'ō (*M. apicalis*), last seen in 1837; Bishop's ō'ō (*M. bishopi*), native to Maui and Moloka'i, last seen on Moloka'i in 1904; the Hawaii ō'ō (*M. nobilis*), last seen in 1934.

69. Passenger Pigeon. From flocks with a billion or more members in the early 19th century, the last passenger pigeon, Martha, died in the Cincinnati Zoo in 1914.

70. Perrin's Cave Beetle. Discovered in 1905, along with several beetle corpses. If it is extinct, water pollution could be a cause. Epigram quoted in W.G. Sebald's *The Rings of Saturn*.

See "Observations on the Natural History of Diving Beetles" by James G. Needham and Helen V. Williamson, *American Naturalist*, vol 41 (488), August 1907, pp. 477-94.

"*Marvelous fellow*": see M. K. Herbert's "In Contemplation of a Diving Beetle," *Interdisciplinary Studies for Literature and the Environment*, 1997, 4(2), 101.

Originally described by entomologist Abeille de Perrin, there is no evidence this beetle ever lived in a cave.

71.   Pig-footed Bandicoot. Last collected in 1901 and last seen in the 1950s, extinction probably due to changing Aboriginal fire regimes (burning the dry grass allowed new shoots to grow, which the bandicoot thrived on), and possibly introduced cats.

Creation story from "Singing Subjects and Sacred Objects: More on Munn's Transformation of Subjects into Objects in Central Australian Mythology" by John Morton, *Oceania*, volume 58, #2, Dec 1987, pp. 100-18.

72.   Po'ouli. Several factors are thought to be responsible for the po'ouli's extinction, including habitat loss, avian malaria, predation by pigs, rats, cats and mongooses (all introduced species), and decline of tree snails, their primary food source. The last one died in 2004.

73.   Pyrenean Ibex. In 2009, the Pyrenean ibex became the first species to be cloned. A living offspring was produced, however it died only minutes later due to lung failure, so the species arguably went extinct twice.

A series of linked factors that each affect the population as described in the text is known as an extinction vortex.

Much of the description is based on *Short Stalks; Or Hunting Camps, North, South, East and West*, by Edward North Buxton, published by Edward Stanford (London) and G. P. Putnam's Sons (New York), 1892. Additional information from "Distribution, status and conservation problems of the Spanish Ibex, *Capra pyrenaica* (Mammalia: Artiodactyla)," Perez, J.M., Granados, J.E., Soriguer, R.C., Fandos, P., Marquez, F.J., and Crampe, J.P., *Mammal Rev.* 2002, Volume 32, No. 1, 26–39 and "The Gemshorn: A Reconstruction," Horace Fitzpatrick, *Proc. of the Royal Musical Assoc.*, volume 99, (1972-73), pp. 1-14.

74.   Rabb's Fringe-limbed Tree Frog. Another victim of the chytrid fungus. Joe Mendelson, Curator of Herpetology in Zoo Atlanta has lamented that herpetologists have become "forensic taxonomists" for how rapidly species are becoming extinct after they are discovered.

75.   Red-bellied Gracile Mouse Opossum. As described, the red-bellied gracile mouse opossum was a victim of habitat destruction because its forest was logged for cattle ranching and sugar cane.

76. Ridley's Stick Insect. Known from only one specimen, collected in Singapore in 1904. When Alfred Russell Wallace visited Singapore in 1854, he remarked that if the present deforestation continued, "countless tribes of interesting insects [would] become extinct." (Writing to Edward Newman, 9 May 1854, as reproduced in *Letters from the Malay Archipelago*, Oxford University Press, 2013.)

The status of this species is uncertain because Henry Nicholas Ridley, Director of the Singapore Botanic Gardens, found the specimen on an orchid in the Orchid House of the Gardens. Because it is similar to some African stick insects, it may have been an imported "alien," but there was at least one case of a local stick insect that found its way in, so it could be a member of a now extinct species.

77. Rocky Mountain Locust. The last major swarms were between 1873 and 1877.

78. Rodrigues Solitaire. Not nearly as famous as the dodo from neighboring Mauritius, the solitaire also nested on the ground and suffered when imported cats and pigs preyed on its eggs and chicks. It is thought to have become extinct between the 1730s and 1760s.

Excerpts from *Lost Land of the Dodo: The Ecological History of Mauritius, Réunion and Rodrigues*, by Anthony Cheke and Julian P. Hume, A and C Black, London, pp. 167-8.

79. Round Island Burrowing Boa. Last seen on Round Island, a tiny islet north of Mauritius, in 1975. Began to decline after the introduction of goats and rabbits in 1840 because of damage to vegetation that caused heavy soil erosion and deterioration of its palm forest habitat.

The line "seeking hospitality from out the dark door of the secret Earth" is from the poem "Snake" by D.H. Lawrence, though it is unknown if this snake sunned itself.

80. Sardinian Pika. Probably migrated to Sardinia during the Pliocene (2-5 million years ago) when lower sea levels due the ice age led to the emergence of a land bridge between Tuscany and the Corsica-Sardinia massif. Last observed in 1774; extinction due to habitat loss, predation and competition from introduced alien species, including hares, goats and foxes.

"Guardians of time" were characters in Sardinian writer Sergio Afzeni's 1996 novel *Lightly We Passed on Earth*. Some of the language in this piece is inspired by D.H. Lawrence's *Sea and Sardinia*. See also "Sardinian Pika," in *Làcanas*, no. 52, Sept-Oct, 2011.

81. Scrawny Stubfoot Toad. Like the Andean black toad, a member of the genus of true toads, known as harlequin or stubfoot toads, found in the neotropics from Costa Rica to Bolivia. Most of the species in the genus *Atelopus*, known as harlequin frogs, have

suffered dramatic declines due to the chytrid fungus, compounded by climate change, which has caused droughts in protected areas. This species has not been recorded since 1989.

Description based on James A Peters' "The Frog Genus *Atelopus* in Ecuador (Anura: Bufonidae)," *Smithsonian Contributions to Zoology*, 1973, Number 145, 27-30.

In Renard's story, toads are deemed ugly.

82. Schomburgk's Deer. Had limited range in southeast Asia, primarily in Thailand. Lost habitat to commercial rice production in the 19th century and was hunted for the supposed medicinal or magical properties of its majestic antlers. The last individual died in 1938. The only known mounted specimen is in Paris's Muséum National d'Histoire Naturelle, in the Room of Endangered and Extinct Species. The language in the piece was influenced by Juan José Arreola's poem "Deer," which appears in *Models of the Universe: An Anthology of the Prose Poem*, edited by Stuart Friebert and David Young, from which the last line is also taken.

83. Sea Mink. Hunted to extinction, the last known individual died in 1880.

84. Shrub Frogs of Sri Lanka. Etymology of most species from "The Sri Lankan Shrub-Frogs of the Genus *Philautus* Gistel, 1848 (Ranidae: Rhacophorinae), with Description of 27 New Species," Manamendra-Arachchi, K. and Pethiyagoda, R., *The Raffles Bulletin of Zoology*, Supplement 12: 163-303, 2005.

  The quotation and description for *P. zal* is from the above paper and is a quote by the pianist Arthur Rubinstein. The remaining extinct species are *Philautus adspersus, P. halyi, P. hypomelas, P. leocorhinus, P. stellatus, P. temporalis, P. travancoricus, P. variabilis,* and *P. zimmeri.*

85. Spectacled Cormorant. Discovered on the Bering Expedition, led by Vitus Bering, which successfully mapped the north east part of Asia. Bering's ship was wrecked at the end of 1741 and to survive the winter on a nearby island, the sailors began to eat the cormorants, following the Kamchatkan method of encasing the bird in clay with all of its feathers then baking it in a heated pit. The results of this method were a juicy meal, according to Steller. News of the expedition about the local wildlife, including sea otters, brought fur traders who extensively hunted the birds, considering it a tasty delicacy.

86. Steller's Sea Cow. Extinction in 1768 due to overhunting, only 27 years after its discovery by Europeans. See Ann Forsten and Phillip Youngman's entry for "Hydrodamalis gigas" in *Mammalian Species* no. 165, pp. 1-3, as well as David Day's poem "Siren Song," in *Nevermore: A Book of Hours,* Quattro Books, 2011.

87. Tahitian Sandpiper. The last specimen was recorded in 1777, though the species could have survived into the 19th century. Extinction due to predation from introduced rats.

88. Tecopa Pupfish. Last collected in 1970; extinction due to habitat destruction.

89. Thylacine. Hunted ruthlessly to extinction in Australia in the 1930s. Several video compilations exist on YouTube showing the last thylacines in zoos.

90. Turquoise-throated Puffleg. No confirmed reports since 1976 so classed as Possibly Extinct due to habitat destruction.

   Luisa Igloria's poem, found in her book of the same title published by Utah State University Press (2014), is based on the essay "Joyas Volardores" by Brian Doyle, published in *American Scholar*, Autumn 2004.

91. Toolache Wallaby. According to the Australian Government, hunting of the toolache wallaby reduced its numbers, but the main cause of extinction was conversion of habitat to agriculture. Became rare by 1924; the last survivor died in captivity in 1939.

   Description based on *Extinct and Vanishing Animals of the Old World* by Francis Harper, 1945, New York, American Committee for International Wildlife Protection.

92. Twenty-Four Rayed Sunstar. This sunstar, a species of starfish, suffered from the effects of overfishing compounded with an unusually strong El Niño event, which warmed the oceans. It hasn't been seen in the Galapagos Islands since 1983.

93. Ukrainian Migratory Lamprey. Formerly found in the Dniestr, Dniepr and Don river drainages in the Ukraine, lampreys are jawless fish and the oldest vertebrates on Earth, dating back to more than 400 million years ago. Despite their physical similarity to eels (which have been around less than 60 million years), they are more closely related to sharks and hagfish. Extinction possibly due to overhunting. About half of the remaining 38 species of lampreys are parasitic, feeding by boring into fish flesh and sucking their blood.

94. Ula-ai-Hawane. Last seen in 1892. Quote is from R.C. L. Perkins, *Vertebrata* (1903). In: *Fauna Hawaiiensis, or the Zoology of the Sandwich Islands*, Vol. 1 Part 4. Cambridge University Press: Cambridge, p. 405.

95. Urania Sloanus. Sometimes called the most beautiful moth in the world, *U. sloanus* was last seen in 1894 or 1895 in Jamaica. Extinction due to habitat loss and loss of one of its larval food plants. The quote is from Lady Edith Blake and the piece is based on descriptions by her and Philip Henry Gosse. (Edith Blake, 1892 *Urania sloanus, North American Review*, vol 154, pp. 343-52; Philip Henry Gosse, *The Romance of Natural History*, 1861, Gould and Lincoln, Boston, republished electronically by Arment Biological Press, 2000.)

96. Wake Island Rail. Wake Island is in the north Pacific Ocean, 3,700 kilometers west of Honolulu. The Wake Island rail was last seen by starving Japanese troops who were stranded on the small island during the Second World War.

See "The extinct Wake Island Rail Gallirallus wakensis: a comprehensive species account based on museum specimens and archival records," by Storrs L. Olson and Mark J. Rauzon, *Wilson Journal of Ornithology*, 123(4), pp. 663-89.

97. Western Black Rhinoceros. Inspired by a similar essay in Eliot Weinberger's *An Elemental Thing* published in 2007 by New Directions. Kaoru Maruyana's poem "A Rhinoceros and a Lion " was published in May 1956 in *Poetry Magazine*.

98. Xerces Blue Butterfly. First described in 1852 by Jean Baptiste Boisduval, the Xerces blue had a small range in the dunes of what is now the Sunset District of San Francisco. It is believed to be the first butterfly to become extinct due to habitat loss caused by urban development and was last seen in the early 1940s. The piece was inspired by the poem "Advice to a Butterfly" by Maxwell Bodenheim, and haiku by Issa.

99. Yunnan Lake Newt. Last seen in 1979. Extinction related to general habitat degradation from pollution, land reclamation and duck farming, as well as the introduction of exotic fish and frog species.

100. Zanzibar Leopard. Searches for leopards on the island in the 1990s turned up no individuals—it was hunted to extinction, primarily during the 1960s during a widespread anti-witchcraft campaign. See "Chasing imaginary leopards: science, witchcraft and the politics of conservation in Zanzibar" by Martin Walsh and Helle Goldman, *Journal of East Africa Studies*, vol 6, no. 4, 2012, pp. 727-46. Yoruba hunter poems can be found in *The Rattle Bag*, edited by Seamus Heaney and Ted Hughes, Faber and Faber, 1982.

Daniel Hudon, originally from Canada, is a lecturer in astronomy, physics, maths, and writing. He lives and works in Boston. He is the author of a nonfiction book, *The Bluffer's Guide to the Cosmos* (Oval Books, UK) and two chapbooks—*Evidence for Rainfall* and *The Hole in the Kitchen Floor* (both Pen & Anvil).

Links to his writing and information about his work as an educator can be found at www.danielhudon.com. Connect with him on Twitter @daniel_hudon.